TV MISTAKES

Jon Sandys

TED SMART

First published in Great Britain in 2004 by
Virgin Books Ltd
Thames Wharf Studios
Rainville Road
London
W6 9HA

A catalogue record for this book is available from the British Library.

This book produced for
The Book People Ltd
Hall Wood Avenue
Haydock
St Helens
WA11 9UL

ISBN 0 7535 0924 5

Typeset by Phoenix Photosetting, Chatham, Kent
Printed and bound in Great Britain by Bookmarque

CONTENTS

ACKNOWLEDGEMENTS

Many thanks must go to the members and visitors of moviemistakes.com for helping to submit and check many of the entries in this book – one pair of eyes only goes so far! A special thanks to Yoshi, jle, Shay, princesskelli, MAC, pinkwafer, Sereenie and David Mercier.

Also huge thanks to my family and friends for being supportive/ mocking as needed, to keep me motivated, but also to keep my otherwise unrestrained mistake-spotting in check.

ABOUT THE SITE AND THE AUTHOR

First and foremost, please don't think I've spotted all of these mistakes myself. While I'll gladly admit I've got *slightly* geeky tendencies, locking myself into a darkened room for days on end purely to catch every small-screen blunder possible would be taking it too far. They've been submitted by myself and many, many other keen-eyed viewers from around the world to my website, moviemistakes.com. Initially, as the name suggests, it was all about films, but over time more and more people were keen to submit things they'd spotted in their favourite TV shows, so I took the plunge, opened my virtual doors to them, and was stunned at the response.

moviemistakes.com has grown far beyond my wildest expectations. It was initially started as a random hobby, in fact more of an experiment, just to see if I could make a basic web page. For a long time it was getting a few hundred hits a day, and even that was over and above anything I'd expected. At the time of writing the site gets around 30,000 visitors a day and, depending on just how many mistakes are found in the latest releases, traffic can get as high as 100,000 people a day.

Much like mistakes in films, finding little things we've missed in our favourite TV programmes isn't meant to be criticism or an exercise in finger-pointing, but more a sign of just how often we watch and re-watch the shows that we love. To me and most mistake-spotters, finding inconsistencies in television programmes, be it continuity or characters' backgrounds, is purely a product of how involved we get in the shows. Having said that, when the writers forget a point which even the most casual fan could have reminded them of, it does occasionally make you wonder . . .

HOW ARE MISTAKES MADE?

In the case of TV shows, often it's down to rapidity of shooting. Although there's no universal schedule, a two-hour film can take months to shoot, while many half-hour shows do their principal filming in one evening, and then make use of the takes they have. As such, TV shows are slightly less prone to the large-scale film errors caused by one scene being shot over several days, but far more prone to minor movement changes caused by cutting multiple takes into one scene. Keep a close eye on the hand, arm and leg movements of people in your favourite programme the next time you're watching, and you may surprise yourself.

Aside from the 'standard' continuity mistake, TV programmes are prone to a very media-specific lapse, namely the changing past of various characters. Your average film is fairly self-contained: two hours of linear development, starting with complete strangers, and the writers can do what they like with them – even if they come back in a sequel there's not all that much back story to worry about. However, while TV shows also start with fresh characters, they can then have ten years or more of 'life' and, as reading this book will show you, the fans **remember,** whether it's changing birthdays, forgotten skills, or homes that redesign themselves.

And, of course, they're just as prone as everything else to reflections of crew being caught when they shouldn't be, and boom mikes swinging into shot. Also, shows that consistently use the same set can run into problems on the occasions that a different angle is needed, and they need to use temporary walls or other concealing features to hide bits of the set which aren't normally seen.

ABOUT THIS BOOK

Like *Movie Mistakes* before it, this book isn't meant to be used as a step-by-step guide to finding mistakes, so while the episodes are in the order they were shown, mistakes within episodes aren't necessarily chronological. Mistake-spotting is fun, but shouldn't become obsessive!

The mistakes listed were picked according to their own merits, rather than covering as many episodes as possible, so if your favourite episode apparently has no mistakes in it, it's almost certainly because people haven't spotted or contributed many yet, not that it's perfect (although you never know . . .)

Also like *Movie Mistakes*, all the entries in this book have been submitted and checked by visitors and members of moviemistakes.com. However, occasionally different versions of episodes are shown on TV or released on DVD, and the DVD/video versions can be cropped differently, revealing more or less of the screen. Ultimately many things are prone to interpretation, so if you've got a different take on anything here, I'm happy to be argued with!

CHANGING THE COURSE OF HISTORY

These are mistakes which even the least keen-eyed fans become aware of, as they're almost entirely plot-driven rather than visual. Character traits and experiences which are seemingly set in stone in some episodes can then radically change later if the plot demands it. Of course it's not real, but sometimes things can be a little *too* different . . .

Boy Meets World

The Fugitive
Alan says Cory and Shawn have been best friends since Shawn taught Cory how to pick the lock on his playpen. But the flashback in 'It's Not You, It's Me' shows Shawn and Cory meeting for the first time at the zoo, aged around six or seven.

The Double Lie
In this episode, Alan says Eric was four in 1978. That would mean that Eric would be twenty in 1994. But Eric is driving in 1993 at sixteen.

What I Meant to Say
Mr Feeny's office in this episode is the same room used as the janitor's closet in 'Janitor Dad'.

Fishing for Virna
When the three kids spill the milk, Chet comes out of a door marked 'Custodian' but in earlier episodes that door was marked 'Girls' for the girls' bathroom.

No Such Thing as a Sure Thing

In this episode, and a few others, it's stated that Topanga's mother's name is Rhiannon, yet in earlier episodes Topanga said that her mother's name was Chloe.

Show Me the Love

Shawn says that his mom left home when he was nine, but in the early seasons, his mom is still home, and takes off during Season Two or Three, when Shawn is about fourteen.

Buffy the Vampire Slayer

I Robot, You Jane

Buffy's birth date starts at 1979. In this episode, when the demon pulls up Buffy's file in the school system, it shows her year of birth as 1979 and that she is a senior. But when her file comes up on the student's computer screen, it has changed to 1980 and sophomore. It wasn't until towards the end of Season One in 'Nightmares' that her birth year is revealed as 1981 (on her tombstone before she comes out as a vampire).

The I in Team

Buffy tells Maggie Walsh that she's always wanted a pager. But Buffy has had a pager before, seen in 'Never Kill a Boy on the First Date'.

Charmed

Witchstock

The action takes place in 1967, and Penny (Grams) is married to a man named Allen Halliwell who dies. Allen is supposed to be

Penny's 'first husband', Patty's father and the Charmed Ones' grandfather. But it was previously established that Patty's father was named Jack, and he died in 1964.

Family Guy

Death Lives

In the flashback scene where Peter meets Lois's father, Peter openly farts in anxiety. However, it was discovered in the previous season, when Peter gets his breast examined, that Peter had gas for the first time when he was 30. In this season, it is noted that Peter and Lois have been married for seventeen years, and that Peter is 42. That would make Peter at most 25 when he farts in front of his father-in-law-to-be. Therefore, Peter has been farting for some undisclosed time.

Stuck Together, Torn Apart

This episode explains that Stewie's head became that weird shape from banging it on the roof. But as seen in earlier episodes showing his birth, his head has always been that shape.

Friends

Across whole show

Ross remains the same age (29) across Seasons Three to Five. In Season Three he tells Chandler 'no thanks, I'm 29' when offered chocolate milk, in Season Four when the guys try to party without Gandalf they all say they're 29, and in Season Five when he's trying to reconcile with Emily he says either he does reconcile or he would get divorced for the second time before the age of 30.

The One where Monica Gets a Roommate
The guy who Rachel left at the altar is called Barry Finkel in this episode. In all the other episodes his name is Barry Farber.

The One where Nana Dies Twice
Rachel tells Chandler that she thought he was gay until he spent Phoebe's entire birthday party talking to her breasts. But at this point, since Rachel joined the group, Phoebe hasn't had a birthday; that occurs some episodes later, in 'The One with Two Parts'.

The One where Rachel Finds Out
Rachel recalls how Ross considered asking her on a date on her first night in the city. However, the incident actually occurs (in the pilot episode) on her *second* night in New York.

The One with the Flashback
The action takes place one year before the pilot (Rachel was supposed to get married in one year in the flashback and the pilot started on the day of her wedding). But, in this episode, Ross finds out that Carol is a lesbian. However, not until the second or third episode does he find out she's pregnant. For this to make sense, either she had a really long pregnancy or else they continued sleeping together for a year after she came out (not likely).

The One with the Dirty Girl
In the very first episode, Chandler says that between him and Joey they haven't had a relationship that lasted longer than a Mento. In this episode, however, we find out that Joey went out with Angela Delveccio for three years.

The One with All the Resolutions

In 'The One with the Baby on the Bus' (Season Two) Phoebe names several of the chords which she can play on the guitar. Then in this episode she states 'I don't know the actual names of the chords' when teaching Joey how to play the guitar.

The One with the Kips

In this episode, they say the reason Kip was phased out was because he dated Monica and they broke up badly. However, in the first season (in 'Dozen Lasagnes') Chandler says Kip left because he got married. Also, Joey knows all about Kip in the 'Dozen Lasagnes' episode, even though he was gone before Joey arrived; now in this season, for some reason Rachel knows about Kip but Joey doesn't.

The One with the Joke

In 'The One with the Chicken Pox' Monica says she always has to sleep on one side of the bed (the right, as we look at it). In this episode she is sleeping on the opposite side. Considering how obsessive she is this change just doesn't ring true.

The One where Chandler Doesn't Like Dogs

It's mentioned a number of times in this episode that Ross doesn't like ice cream. But in the episode where Ross spends time with Marcel when the monkey is in the movie, there is a scene in which Ross and Marcel are walking down the street and Ross has an ice-cream cone. Marcel starts to eat it, and then Ross laughs and throws it away. Why would he care if the monkey licked his ice cream if he didn't like it to begin with?

The One with Rachel's Assistant

Ross has always said that Carol was his first (and only, until Julie) sexual partner, but in the episode where they tell each other's secrets Chandler says Ross slept with the cleaner when they were at college. Some people say that Ross had kept it a secret, and that's why it had never come out before, but considering that he categorically states several times over Seasons One and Two how he'd only EVER been with Carol, getting quite upset at times, that explanation just doesn't ring true.

The One After 'I do'

Chandler and Ross are surprised to notice that Joey has very small feet. At least Chandler – who, apart from being his best friend, has been his flatmate for eight years – should know Joey's shoe size.

The One with the Secret Closet

The whole show is about Monica's secret closet (the one near the bathroom), why she keeps the door locked and how Chandler wants to find out what's in there. However, in 'The One with the Dozen Lasagnes', the door is open and the closet reveals nothing more than clothes and other regular stuff you put in a closet. Also in the one where Phoebe and Rachel are looking for Christmas presents ('The One with the Routine') Rachel says she'll go and check the back closet, the one next to the bathroom.

The One where Emma Cries

In Season Four ('The One with Joey's New Girlfriend') Gunther is pretending to collect birth dates, and Ross starts saying 'mine's December the . . .' before being cut off. However, in this episode (Season Nine) Ross says his is on 18 October.

In the coffee house, when Ross and Joey are having a fight about Joey's proposal to Rachel, Ross does the 'quote gesture' with his hands and Joey says he doesn't know what this means. Back in Season Eight though ('The One with the Secret Closet') Joey has used it himself when talking to Chandler, in the scene where he asks him to bring a bobby pin to pick the closet's lock.

The One with Phoebe's Birthday Dinner

In this episode we hear that Phoebe's birthday is around Halloween – 31 October. However, in 'The One with Frank Jr' in Season Three, she tells Frank that her birthday is 16 February.

The One with Rachel's Other Sister

Phoebe tells Joey he doesn't know how to lie and that he doesn't sound convincing. However, in 'The One with the Soap Opera Party' Joey lies to the guys and they buy it, also he says that he's been doing it for years.

The One with the Sharks

Phoebe talks to Joey about how he's never been in a long-term relationship. He has been, though – with Angela Delveccio – with whom he went out for three years, as we found out in 'The One with the Dirty Girl'.

M*A*S*H

Across whole show

In the early episodes, Col. Blake's wife is named Mildred; later her name is changed to Lorraine.

In the first season of *M*A*S*H*, Hawkeye mentions that his father lives in Vermont, in the later seasons his father lives in

Crab Apple Cove, Maine and has never left there in thirty years.

M*A*S*H – The Pilot

Hawkeye and Trapper are going to send Ho Jon to the States to go to medical school. Hawkeye says Ho Jon can stay with his parents, but throughout the rest of the series Hawkeye's father is a widower.

Sometimes You Hear the Bullet

As Frank receives his Purple Heart, Henry calls him 'Franklin D. Burns'. All other references to his full name in the series give his middle name as 'Marion'.

Hot Lips and Empty Arms

Margaret is in Henry's office drunk and she tells Henry that he looks just like her father did before he died. In Season Nine, episode four ('Father's Day') Margaret's father, Alvin 'Howitzer' Houlihan, visits her at the 4077.

Radar's Report

The psychiatrist is called Milton Freedman in this episode and Sydney Freedman in all other episodes in which he appears (always the same psychiatrist – being played by the same actor).

Abyssinia, Henry

When Frank learns he is to take command of the MASH, he says, 'I just wish I'd taken ROTC in school'. However, in Season Two, episode two ('Five O-Clock Charlie') he says that he learned gunnery in the ROTC.

The General Flipped at Dawn

Actress Lynnette Mettey was introduced in 'Carry on Hawkeye' (Season Two) as Lt Anderson, but in this episode her character's name changes to Nurse Baker.

Fade Out, Fade In (60 mins.)

In the episode 'Chief Surgeon Who' (Season One), near the end we see Radar in Col. Blake's office smoking a cigar with ease, but in this episode when Col. Potter offers Radar a cigar, he doesn't know how to smoke it and he throws up after he puffs it.

Only Fools and Horses

Sleepless in Peckham

In 'The Frog's Legacy' (1987 special), Del and Rodney learned the story of Freddy The Frog for the first time – neither of them had ever heard of him before (Aunt Irene explains to Del who Freddy was. She mentions both 'Freddy The Frog' and his real name 'Frederick Robdal'. Del has heard of neither of these names.) Yet, in this episode, it would seem that Del had known Freddy since he was fifteen. He even went on their first Jolly Boys' Outing with the rest of the gang.

Red Dwarf

Across whole show

In some episodes, we are told there were originally 169 crew members on board the ship. In others it is 1169. For example, in the episode 'Confidence and Paranoia', Lister says there were 169 crewmen on Red Dwarf before the accident. By the episode 'Justice', Rimmer is accused of murdering 1167 people on the Red Dwarf crew.

Me2

Rimmer says that Lister constantly annoyed him for two years, but in Series One, episode four, 'Waiting for God', Lister said he had only been on Red Dwarf for eight months.

The End

In this, the very first episode, Lister runs his arm through Rimmer and he remains unchanged. Whenever anything passes through him in the rest of the series, he fades.

Beyond a Joke

Lister screws Kryten's head around only once to get it on but in 'Tikka to Ride' he had to do it several times to get it on.

Ouroboros

In the first ever episode of *Red Dwarf* ('The End') Lister says that he bought his pet cat, Frankenstein, on Titan, but in this episode he says he bought the cat while on Mimas.

Seinfeld

The Wife

When Kramer is asked about urinating in the shower, he replies 'I take baths.' But in the episode with the low-flow shower heads, Kramer is disgusted by taking a bath, saying he was 'lying in a tepid pool of my own filth'.

The Comeback

In 'The Suicide', Kramer discusses suicide with Jerry, and says that he'd give someone 72 hours to come out of a coma before all his property is up for grabs. However, in this episode, Kramer tells Jerry that he never knew that people could come out of a coma.

Simpsons, The

New Kid on the Block

Bart says his home address is 1094 Evergreen Terrace. In 'Homer The Vigilante', his home address is 723 Evergreen Terrace; and for the rest of the series, it is 742 Evergreen Terrace.

And Maggie Makes Three

Bart comments on Homer's extreme reaction when he realised Marge was pregnant with Maggie. In the next flashbacks, when Homer reacts in the same way to hearing about Bart and Lisa, they are shown in the house at Evergreen Terrace both times. In Season Four, in 'Lisa's First Word', it is shown that the Simpsons did not move to Evergreen Terrace until just before Lisa was born. Other episodes have also shown that Homer was with Marge at Doctor Hibbert's when she found out about her other pregnancies.

Fear of Flying

Marge has a problem with flying, but in 'Mr Lisa goes to Washington' in Season Three, they travel there by plane and Marge appears to be OK during the flight.

Half-Decent Proposal

Artie Ziff is upset to discover that Marge is married. But not only does he address her as 'Marge Simpson' and not 'Marge Bouvier' at first, but five seasons ago he met Homer and Marge at a school reunion and Homer said that Marge was his wife.

Star Trek: Voyager

Flashback

It seems that the producers didn't watch *Star Trek VI*. In the scene where Mr Tuvok explains to Captain Janeway about the explosion of the Klingon moon, he says that Captain Kirk and Dr McCoy were arrested two days after the explosion; in the film it actually happened over two months after the explosion.

Scientific Method

At one point Seven goes into the turbolift and she says 'Deck 5'. When the turbolift doors open she gets out and walks to the Mess Hall to pour a cup of coffee. How can she be in the Mess Hall if she is on Deck 5? The Mess Hall has been previously established to be on Deck 2, right below the bridge.

That '70s Show

Trampled Under Foot

Kelso is wearing a T-shirt with Dirty Harry on it saying 'Go Ahead, Make My Day'. *Sudden Impact* was the first Dirty Harry movie to use that expression and that film didn't come out until 1983.

NOW THAT WAS JUST PLAIN BAD

'Bad acting' could be putting it a bit harshly, but these entries are ones where the actors involved have perhaps let their concentration slip and apparently overlooked certain points during filming. Whether it's moving while 'dead', making 'accidents' a little too obvious, or overlooking events which are obvious to the audience, even the best actors can lapse on occasion . . .

24

Day 2: 5:00 A.M.–6:00 A.M.

Kim drops the phone in order to shoot Matheson, then she picks it up again. Jack then tells Kim to shoot him again, so she drops the phone first, shoots him, and when she picks the phone up for the second time it is upside down. Kim is talking into the earpiece, but Jack and Kim seem to have no problem continuing the conversation.

Band of Brothers

Carentan

When the allied soldiers run into the city, one of them gets shot and falls to the ground in the middle of the street. Yet in the very next shot of that location, you can see the 'dead' soldier adjust his arm.

Buffy the Vampire Slayer

Never Kill a Boy on the First Date

In the famous scene where Buffy tells Giles, 'If the Apocalypse comes, beep me', she grabs her pager from out of shot. Trouble is, she's standing in the middle of her hall and there's nowhere she could have picked the gadget up from.

Gone

An invisible Buffy is typing on the social worker's keyboard and the letter 'B' is pressed several times. Seconds later, when she prints what she's been typing, it's revealed to be 'All work and no play make Nancy a dull girl', a phrase which contains no Bs.

Villains

Dawn returns from school and goes up to Willow and Tara's room where she finds Tara lying dead on the floor. When Buffy comes in and comforts her, you can see Tara's chest moving as she takes a breath.

Charmed

Sleuthing with the Enemy

When Cole/Belthazar grabs Phoebe to use her as a hostage, you can see, very obviously, that he doesn't pull her. Phoebe actually steps in front of him willingly, despite the look of fear on her face.

The Importance of Being Phoebe

Phoebe is lying on the ground and is supposed to be unconscious; as Cole goes to pick her up Phoebe throws her arms around his neck.

Witchstock

Robin falls over backwards after Paige dumps a canister of marbles onto the floor. But Robin wasn't moving at all when this happened. Trying to walk over marbles will make you fall. But falling while standing still as marbles roll around and bounce off your feet? Not so much.

Friends

The One where They're Going to PARTY!

Phoebe is looking at the front page of the *Chelsea Reporter*. Monica says her restaurant review is on the back page. However, Phoebe doesn't turn to the back page, but merely flips the paper over, looking at the bottom of the front page (and finding the review there).

The One with All the Resolutions

Ross goes into Ben's room to kiss him goodnight. While he's in there, Monica and Chandler leave to do 'laundry'; Phoebe also exits, leaving Joey and Rachel to have their dialogue. Ross is in Ben's room for a long time but, worst of all, he doesn't hear Joey and Rachel's shouting, which he really should have as the door is less than fifteen metres away and can easily be heard through as we've seen on several occasions before.

The One with the Inappropriate Sister

While Phoebe is collecting for charity outside the shop, a man puts a dollar in the bucket and tries to make change for the bus. When Phoebe argues with the man he says, 'Bite me blondie', but he couldn't have known that she is blonde because she has a Santa hat on that covers her entire head and no hair is coming out from underneath the hat.

The One where Chandler Doesn't Like Dogs

Monica and Chandler go to Ross's apartment to use the oven. Monica claims to be able to see the dog which is sitting on the sofa between Joey and Rachel in Monica's apartment. This doesn't seem possible since Ross's apartment is one floor lower than Monica's and even if the window is very low, there is a wall outside around the balcony, which we have seen many times before as well as in this episode.

The One with Rachel's Other Sister

Joey and Phoebe are talking while Rachel and Amy are fighting. As Phoebe says the line 'Oh my God. Shouldn't we do something?' Joey is mouthing her lines.

Monty Python's Flying Circus

Full Frontal Nudity

In the 'buying a bed' sketch, Mr Verity says that the couple 'said mattress twice'. Because of his affliction – that he is compelled to multiply all numbers by ten – he should have said 'twenty times'.

Murder, She Wrote

Sing a Song of Murder

In the first scene at Emma's hideaway it is obvious that the two characters Emma and Jessica were filmed separately on the couch and then the film was put together (as both are played by Angela Lansbury). However, Jessica did a lot of moving while she was talking, so Emma was looking straight across at where she had been, despite her bending down as she talked.

Red Dwarf

Balance of Power

The cigarette butts that Lister supposedly tips out of his lager can were clearly in between his hand and the can, and not in the can at all.

Waiting for God
After the cat priest dies on the bed, watch him move his foot so Lister can sit on the edge.

Bodyswap
When The Cat drops the tape of Lister's mind into his cup of tea, Lister can briefly be seen starting to smile. The shot moves quickly away from his face to hide this, but it's still visible.

Marooned
Lister proposes to burn the book *Lolita* (to try and keep warm). Rimmer says to save page 61, but Lister rips out the left-hand page, which would be page 60.

Quarantine
Lister demonstrates the luck virus with the deck of cards but only shuffles the top few cards, then draws the four aces from the bottom of the deck.

Gunmen of the Apocalypse
At the start of the episode, Lister is seen in black and white talking to Loretta. A wider shot shows what's really happening: he is playing on the AR console. In the doorway behind him, Kryten's hand can be seen sticking out. He is supposed to rush in and start talking, but he can be seen waiting off camera to be told when to enter the room.

Legion
When Legion stabs his left hand, everyone grabs and shakes their left hands – except Lister, who grabs and shakes his right hand.

Tikka to Ride

Lister screws in Kryten's replacement head (the one without the 'guilt chip') in exactly the same direction – clockwise – that he *unscrewed* the original head.

Back in the Red (3)

The first time that Lister, The Cat, Kochanski and Kryten are seen in the AR machine, The Cat opens his eyes, realises that it is not in the script, smiles, and then closes them.

WE CAN SEE YOU

Television is a very different format to film, but still needs many people behind the scenes to make things work, and for all their talent, every so often they crop up where they're really not meant to be . . .

24

11:00 P.M.–12:00 Midnight

At about 11.30 p.m., just when Jack is preparing to take his first shots at the Drazens as they are running towards the speed-boat, a cameraman/technician is visible (wearing a face shield presumably to protect himself from the shots), and also a TV monitor behind Jack's head.

1:00 A.M.–2:00 A.M.

Jack Bauer and his boss are in a building at night with a shooter hidden somewhere. They open a door and look very carefully to the right and to the left before going through. On the right side you can briefly see two crew members and, as the camera pulls forwards, they back up a little so they can't be seen.

7:00 A.M.–8:00 A.M.

After Nina's been shot, she makes it to the barn to call CTU (about 7.10 a.m.). While she's speaking on the phone there's a cameraman visible on the right-hand side.

Black Adder

Plan C: Major Star

During the general's speech about Blackadder's suitability for organising a concert party, look at the entrance to the trench. In one shot you can see a crew member moving a giant cloth. It is mostly the movement you see, but you can also catch a glimpse of the crew member's face.

Buffy the Vampire Slayer

This Year's Girl (1)
In the scene in the woods, where the Scoobies find the demon that Adam has cut open, a boom mike operator is noticeable in the background.

Normal Again
When the demon in the basement throws Dawn into the corner, watch this in freeze frame. As she looks up it's clear that it's not Michelle Trachtenberg but a much older stunt double with darker skin and different make-up.

EastEnders

In the episode on 15 September 2003, Lisa is talking to the hit-man in her apartment. When the camera is on her, she has her hands on her lap, but when the camera focuses on the hitman you can see another arm beside her, in a vertical position, in the mirror behind him – perhaps a boom mike operator.

Fawlty Towers

Gourmet Night
Just after Basil gets the duck from Andre, he tells Manuel to get the trolley. Basil then walks into the door, and the duck goes flying. The arm of the crewman can briefly be seen holding the

door closed. A few seconds later, Manuel comes through the door and stands on the duck. For about five seconds you can see the crewman's face.

Friends

The One with All the Poker

The group are at Ross's place preparing to play a new game of poker. Marcel the monkey is dancing to the music just before they start the game (before Rachel enters). Take a close look at the reflection in the TV screen and you can see the animal trainer directing Marcel – bouncing up and down so the monkey copies him.

The One with the Bullies

Phoebe visits her father Frank's house and there is a little dog outside. She gets back in the car and the dog jumps up the side of it. When the dog finally gets part way through the window, clearly visible, beside Joey's shoulder, is the top of a head belonging to someone who is holding the dog up.

The One with the Prom Video

During the prom video itself, Monica, Rachel and Monica's date Roy are standing in the living room. When Roy leaves the room saying 'I'm gonna kick Chip's ass' the camera follows him out but, as it's turning, the boom mike operator can be seen kneeling on the floor sliding the mike towards the girls.

Malcolm in the Middle

Red Dress

When the kids are wrapping a present for their parents' wedding anniversary, to the left of Lois, a crew member can be seen holding a bucket of water. He hands the red dress to Lois out of it to give the appearance that she found it in the toilet. He quickly gets out of the camera's view.

Flashback
Lois goes into labour with Malcolm and runs outside taking Francis and Reese with her. When Francis says 'You're a liar, you're a liar', the camera and camera operator's reflections can be seen in the back window of the car.

Monty Python's Flying Circus

Intermission
Just after Florence Nightingale gets knocked out, a crew member can be seen behind Michael Palin for a short time.

Red Dwarf

The End
When Lister is telling his door to lock so he can get his cat out, look through the window and you can see the hand of a crew member pushing the door shut.

Better Than Life
As Rimmer gets in the car on the beach, the cameraman's reflection is visible on the side of the car.

Star Trek: The Next Generation

Remember Me
In the scene where Dr Crusher is on the Bridge all alone, immediately before the 'universe' collapses, a cameraman on a boom

is noticeable in the black plastic next to the turbolift, which is behind her.

Unification (2)
Picard, Spock and Data have just escaped from the female Romulan commander. As they walk out of the room, the reflection of a crew member is apparent in the green glass ornament.

THE AMAZING CHANGING WARDROBE

The curse of continuity departments everywhere – clothes. Unfortunately they're always needed except for an, er, certain type of production, which is rather outside the scope of this book. But as soon as people are in specific outfits with specific hair styles, a wrong movement or gust of wind can throw everything out. And even cartoons don't escape . . .

24

8:00 A.M.–9:00 A.M.

In this episode (and during the previous few hours) Kim Bauer is wearing sandals with no socks. At 08.36 when Terri has just been taken from the room where they are being held captive you see a shot of Kim sitting down and she is wearing pink leather slipper-style shoes and black socks. Given that the show's in real time and she's being held captive, there's been no chance for her to change.

Alias

Across whole show

Emily Sloane's left-hand ring finger was shipped to Arvin Sloane in one episode in Season Two. When they are reunited in the Philippines, that finger is bandaged and missing. Later, in the episode when she is shot, and when she tells Arvin the CIA is listening, the left-hand ring finger is back on her hand.

Angel

I Will Remember You

Buffy and Angel are talking in the sewer and Buffy has just a few strands of hair over her shoulder. This changes to her having all her hair on one side, over it, before her hair goes back to how it was.

To Shanshu in L.A.

Near the end of the episode, Angel is fighting Vocah in the mausoleum and Angel rips off Vocah's mask, revealing the maggoty face underneath. In subsequent shots of Angel from behind Vocah, you can still see the edges of the mask on his face, despite it being removed just before.

Disharmony

While Cordelia and Harmony are on the couch talking and drinking, the towel on Cordelia's head is hanging over her shoulder in the long shot, but when we change to a closer shot the towel is now hanging completely behind her.

When Harmony enters Cordelia's bedroom, the strap on Cordelia's top falls down over her arm, but then, after the angle changes, it's suddenly back up on her shoulder.

Willow's hair is over her eye when she says 'Thanks for the affirmation', but when we see her again a second later it's tucked behind her ear, without enough time for her to have moved it.

The Shroud of Rahmon

Angel changes into his vampire face but his teeth don't change into his regular fangs – they just remain his normal teeth.

Untouched

Cordelia bandages Angel in the hotel lobby and puts two pieces of tape on him: one at the base of the gauze and one over the wound itself. However, when he takes his shirt off in his room, he only has the one at the base – the one over the wound has completely disappeared.

The Cautionary Tale of Numero Cinco

While Angel is outside looking for Number 5, he is stabbed in the stomach by a demon. In the next scene Angel returns to Wolfram & Hart right after this happens and he is still wearing the same clothes. He mentions he is still in pain, yet there are no rips or tears in his shirt and no bloodstains from his earlier wounding.

Boy Meets World

Pop Quiz

At the end of this episode, Griff is seen standing with Joey and Frankie. He's wearing a jacket over a pink button-down shirt that has a red collar and red accents. He sees a girl, and there's a shot of Joey, who stands up on the bench and screams at the girl; then, when the camera moves back to Griff, he's wearing a jacket over a plain old faded red shirt. I wonder what happened to the other shirt.

The Honeymooners

At one point, when Topanga is supposedly naked under the cover, you can see a large corner of her bra.

Buffy the Vampire Slayer

Prophecy Girl

During Buffy's rooftop fight with the Master, her shoes change in between shots from white heels, to black boots – when she's kicking him – then back to white heels.

Teacher's Pet
Ms French is eating her bug sandwich, with her sleeves pulled up in the wide shots; but in closer shots more focused on the sandwich, her sleeves are down around her wrists.

Innocence (2)
When Buffy wakes up she is wearing metallic nail polish, yet when she went to sleep she had no nail polish on. Later, in a scene where Buffy is dreaming about her night with Angel, she has the nail polish on again, even though that took place the night before, when she did not have her nails painted.

Phases
Willow is escaping from Oz the werewolf and runs into the library. Giles is there. In the first shot, he isn't wearing his glasses; in the next shot he is; then he isn't – then in the following shot he is.

The Dark Age
At the end of the episode, Buffy complains to Willow and Xander that she will have to blow her allowance on getting the tattoo removed before her mom sees it. Moments later when Buffy is talking to Giles, the tattoo has completely disappeared. Guess her allowance is safe after all.

When She Was Bad
Joyce is driving Buffy to school and she is wearing a pink tank top. At school that day her shirt is white, but the next day at school she is back to wearing the pink outfit.

Anne

Lily's boyfriend is taken into an alternate dimension, where time moves quicker than ours, and is kept there until he is an old man. But when Buffy finds him, she realises who he is because of his tattoo – which has not faded or aged in any way.

As Buffy fights the hell dimension demons her shoes change from trainers to plain pumps in different shots.

Lover's Walk

Spike is threatening Willow at the factory. In the long shots Willow's hair is up over her face, and in the close-ups it isn't.

The Harsh Light of Day

When Buffy catches Parker talking to another girl he stands up to leave and slings his backpack over one shoulder. In the next shot it's over both shoulders.

As Spike grabs the ring of Amara from Harmony, he's still wearing the huge necklace he had thought was the gem, but when he turns around to leave the necklace has disappeared.

Who Are You? (2)

Adam enters the cave and talks to the vampires; he then pulls the head off one of them, but watch as the vampire falls, as his head is still visible when he is falling out of frame.

Checkpoint

After Buffy has accidentally axed the dummy, watch her blindfold. It goes from being pushed up above her forehead on her hair, to being right down by her eyes. This changes between shots.

Out of My Mind
When Buffy, Willow and Dawn are in the bedroom discussing Riley's problems, Dawn's hair shifts from over her shoulder in the long shots to behind her shoulder in the close-ups.

The Gift
Spike is thrown off the tower by Doc but somehow manages to change from black trousers and boots into blue jeans and white shoes in midair. He's back in black by the time he hits the ground.

Once More, with Feeling
During Giles's song, 'Standing', Buffy's hair is loose as we see her training montage. But when she walks up to him at the end and starts to speak, she's taking it out of a bun. She's definitely not just playing with her hair – if you watch carefully you can see a clip or pin of some sort in her hand that has been holding her hair up.

Buffy is wearing a white shirt before she goes off to confront Sweet. Once she gets there and takes off her coat, she is wearing a red shirt.

Selfless
Anya has a flashback to a song she sang at the time of the episode 'Once More, with Feeling'. During this flashback her hair is much longer and a much harsher blonde than it actually was during that episode.

Doctor Who

Revenge of the Cybermen
Quite a few times during this story arc Vogans appear without

their browny gold eye make-up to reveal pink (human-coloured) eyelids when the rest of them is all brown.

EastEnders

Across whole show

While Kelley and Zoe are freezing in the Scottish Highlands together against the burned-out minibus, Zoe's lips change colour back and forth throughout the scene. They go from hypothermia blue to nice and pink just before Zoe and Kelley kiss.

In the episode where Ash has been kicked out by his dad for having a relationship with Shirley, he comes back to pick up his things. When he asks Asif if he's OK, his hair is wet and slicked backwards. He then walks into the next room a few seconds later and it's dry and to the side.

ER

Out of Africa

Coop has to have a dressing put on his face while a burn victim is being treated. In a later scene, he's assisting in the treatment of another patient and the dressing is gone. But a few minutes later, the patient dies and Coop's dressing is back.

Family Guy

There's Something About Paulie

Peter is outside the cinema waiting for Big Fat Paulie and is wearing a tie; however, when he is in the cinema walking up the aisle, it's gone. When he gets out, he is wearing it again.

Brian Does Hollywood (2)
Peter and Lois take Stuey to the hotel. Peter is wearing a blue suit. In the next scene he wears a black suit. Then, as they get called in the audition room, he is wearing his usual: green pants and white shirt.

Father Ted

Good Luck, Father Ted
On the island Terry MacNamee is talking to Father Ted on the phone; his tie is blown over his shoulder. Following a cut to Father Ted, his tie is hanging straight. After another cut, it is back over his shoulder again.

Hell
Father Dougal's hair changes position during the scene in the car, before they go on holiday.

Friends

The One with the Dozen Lasagnes
Just before Rachel lets it slip to Ross that Carol's going to give birth to a boy, she is sitting on the edge of a chair eating a cookie. Watch her dress, it changes back and forth from being undone from the waist up, to only having two buttons open at the top.

The One where Ross Finds Out
When Rachel finds out that Ross and Julie are getting a cat, watch her neck. When she says 'together?' she's not wearing a necklace. There's a cut to Ross and Julie for a fraction of a second, then a cut back to Rachel saying 'both of you?' and

suddenly, she's wearing a necklace. It then disappears again when she says 'isn't that just lovely?'

The One with the Hypnosis Tape
After 'Mrs Knight' sits down with Phoebe's brother in Central Perk, keep an eye on the strap of her handbag. It starts over her shoulder and moves around and changes position at least half a dozen times.

The One with Chandler in a Box
In this episode Rachel is showing Ross all the things she has kept in a shoe box from their relationship. Her hair is tucked behind her ear in most shots, but when she says, 'I keep the gifts that matter', it's all loose, then, in the following shot, it goes back to how it was. Also, in the shot before that line, she's pointing the fossil at Ross, but when it cuts to a front view she's pointing it upwards.

The One with Ross's Wedding, Part 2
In this episode, in England, where Rachel goes to tell Ross she loves him, she leaves her room wearing a brown sleeveless vest, with a cardigan over her shoulders. The cardigan then disappears in all further shots until after Phoebe says 'he's in love with the British chippy'. Her leather jacket also goes from being in her hands to over her arm.

The One with Rachel's Inadvertent Kiss
When Joey is counting the floors of Ross's building (the first time) to find out where Hot Girl lives, he is wearing a black top with a zip. Then he rushes over to Ross's building and is seen walking down the hall and knocking on what he believes to be Hot Girl's door. In these shots he is wearing a dark purple button-up shirt.

Fine, he could have dressed up for her, but as soon as Ross answers the door, Joey is again wearing the black top with a zip.

The One That Could Have Been, Part 2
Rachel is talking to Joey in his apartment. Since she just 'woke up' she looks messy and rumpled. As she talks, her bra strap slips down her arm. In one shot (as she says, 'I'm a horrible person') the strap is all the way down her arm and then in the next shot it is just tucked under her shirt.

The One where Chandler Can't Cry
Rachel's sister Jill goes to Ross's place, intending to make Rachel mad. When Ross goes to Rachel's to talk to her afterwards, she rolls up her sleeves saying, 'I'll give you something to think about.' The next shot is of Ross, followed by one of Rachel whose sleeves are rolled down. Also, her arms are no longer at her sides but crossed in front of her.

The One with the Apothecary Table
In the previous episode 'The One with the Routine' Ross, Monica, Chandler and Janine are dancing at the pre-recorded Millennium party and Monica has her Christmas tree up. After the party, Joey kisses Janine. In this episode, he walks into Monica's apartment and says he just kissed her. However, Monica's tree is down and they have all changed their clothes. Surely if he just kissed her then it is still the night of the party, therefore the tree should be up and Monica, Ross and Joey should be wearing the same clothes from the party.

The One with the Ring
Bruce Willis finally breaks free from his closed-mouth attitude and cries like a baby to Rachel. He wears a white linen shirt that constantly flicks between tear-stained and wrinkled to ironed

and clean while talking to her at the breakfast bar and Rachel is making sexual advances to stop him crying.

The One with Monica's Thunder

I know it's harsh, and I love the show, but it has to be mentioned. This episode carries on immediately from the end of the previous season, with the engagement celebrations continuing. However, in the few minutes that have elapsed, Chandler has somehow lost quite a bit of weight.

The One with the Cheap Wedding Dress

The dress Monica tries on at the expensive store (which she says she'll buy cheaper elsewhere) is not the one she then buys at the discount store.

The One with the Holiday Armadillo

When Ross is on the couch telling Ben about Hanukah, Ben's hair varies from shot to shot. In the first shot it's flat and in the next it's spiked up at the front. His hair stays spiked up for a few shots and then returns to flat.

The One with the Truth About London

When Monica and Chandler are undressing, Chandler takes his clothes off really quickly, and Monica says 'wow, you're fast'. Then they say that they are about to see each other naked. Monica isn't wearing the top of her dress (a two-piece) any more, but she could only have removed that by pulling it over her head, which she hasn't done.

When Rachel goes to Carol's house and tries to tell Ben to stop playing pranks, her bag changes between being on her shoulder and being in her hand in almost every shot.

The One with Monica's Boots

Monica is removing her trainers and replacing them with her boots so it looks as if she was wearing her boots all along. In one shot the left leg of her jeans is tucked into her boots, but when she stands up it is sitting perfectly.

The One with the Stain

Monica falls off a chair and you can see that she is wearing a white bra because some of the cup and the strap is showing (when she says 'you're not getting it'). Towards the end of the episode (still the same day) Rachel points out that Monica has the same bra on as their new cleaner, Brenda. The bra she is meant to have on is 'pink with the lacy cup'. What happened to the white bra she had on a few scenes before?

The One in Barbados, Part 2

When David and Mike are both about to propose to Phoebe, she is talking first to David and then to Mike, and each time the shot changes the amount of hair hanging down Phoebe's back changes from a little to a lot.

The One where Emma Cries

When Rachel wakes up Emma during a nap, against Phoebe's advice, there is a shot of Emma in the cot. She is wearing a plain pink hat, but in the next shot, when Rachel lifts her out of the cot, she is wearing a white hat with what looks like little flowers on it.

The One where No One Proposes

Rachel is in bed feeding Emma and Ross is sitting right beside her. They are talking about their relationship and the future. As the shots alternate between Rachel and Ross it can be seen that Rachel's hair in one shot is in front of her shoulder and in the next it is behind her shoulder. This happens several times.

The One where Rachel Goes Back to Work
Ross bends over Emma to kiss her and gets the bow stuck on his head. Rachel is about to tell him but it is slightly over his eye, making it possible for him to see it. In the next shot, a second later, it has moved to the centre of his forehead.

The One with the Lottery
Chandler is on the phone to find out if he got the job as an advertising intern. He then hangs up and rolls up one of his sleeves. In the next shot of him both sleeves are rolled up. Then his sleeves slip down again, but when it cuts to a closer shot, you can see they're once again rolled up.

The One with the Sharks
Chandler and Monica are talking about his supposed shark obsession after she's bought him the nature video. Chandler's collar switches from up to down depending on the shot. It changes a number of times during the scene.

Futurama

Mother's Day
When the Professor's and Mom's clothes are thrown around the bedroom, their teeth are already out and seen in jars next to the bed. The problem with this is that both of them are 'wearing' their teeth, as can be seen when they talk.

The Deep South
As Fry and Bender are sleeping, the knob on Bender's chest-plate appears out of nowhere.

Why Must I Be a Crustacean in Love
Fry and Zoidberg are fighting and Zoidberg slashes the 'Z' insignia (a tip of the hat to Zorro) onto Fry's shirt, then adds a D and an R. When Fry releases Zoidberg from the nutcrackers and addresses the king, his shirt is repaired.

A Tale of Two Santas
The ripped elves' hats are in perfect condition in the shot taken from behind the sack looking towards Robot Santa but, as the elves run off, the hats become ripped again.

Home Improvement

Insult to Injury
When Tim gets on the steamroller, he is wearing the arm sling. Next shot, and for the remainder of the scene, it is gone.

M*A*S*H

The Ringbanger
After doing his push-ups, Colonel Brighton puts on a red robe and talks with Trapper and Hawkeye. In some shots the cord from the robe's hood is hanging down and in others it is tucked in.

While Frank is trying to examine the Colonel, Buzz's robe is open in some shots and in others it is tied at the waist.

Potter's Retirement

BJ and Hawkeye are trying to find out who snitched on Potter and they search Charles's belongings back at The Swamp. BJ wraps Charles's white scarf around his neck. Once Charles returns to his tent, the scarf changes position several times.

Red Dwarf

Blue

The flashback sequence of Rimmer and Lister searching everyone's lockers is supposed to have happened not long after the accident which killed the crew. Rimmer is wearing his most up-to-date blue hard-light hologram costume, when he actually should have been wearing his standard cream-shirt uniform.

Back in the Red (1)

None of the crew seems to have noticed that Kochanski's hair has grown considerably longer given the fact this episode is set straight after the events that happen in 'Nanarchy'.

Back in the Red (3)

The Cat does his dance with Blue Midget standing behind one of the legs of Blue Midget, and changes his clothes. The old clothes he throws on the ground when changing disappear in the wide shot of the landing area.

Scrubs

My Journey

When Elliot is splashed by the dolphin, watch carefully and you can see that her hair is already wet.

Sex and the City

Attack of the Five Foot Ten Woman

Charlotte is seen running into the sauna with a towel wrapped around her waist. The towel comes loose and is nearly falling off, but in the next shot it is neatly tied around her waist.

Boy, Interrupted

At the end of the show, when Carrie visits Jeremy at the psychiatric facility, they are sitting outside having a picnic. As they are talking, notice Carrie's necklace. It is a bolero-type and from shot to shot the red stones on the end move up the necklace to near the clasp and then back down into her cleavage. Then they go back up again.

Great Sexpectations

Before Berger passes out on Carrie's bed, he takes off his jacket and sports coat, and even begins unbuttoning his shirt. When the two of them wake up in the morning, Berger's shirt is buttoned up, and his sports jacket is back on. I don't know about you, but when I pass out I don't wake up to put clothes back on.

Simpsons, The

Life on the Fast Lane

While Marge is on the phone to her sisters, her necklace changes from white to red.

Moaning Lisa

Marge is driving Lisa to school. In one shot, you can see that her necklace is red. Then in the next shot it is white. It then changes back to red. When she says, 'Oh Homer, you'd lose your head if it wasn't secured to your neck', her necklace is white. However, when she gives the cupcakes to Homer and Bart, it is red.

The Simpsons Christmas Special: Simpsons Roasting on an Open Fire
Lewis changes colour from black to white when Milhouse dares Bart to pull Santa's beard off.

Bart the Murderer
Bart's bruised eye has healed by the time he reaches Skinner's office to lick envelopes.

At recess, Bart splits his pants in front of the girls. This split isn't visible in any other part of the episode.

Flaming Moe's
Homer drives to Moe's Tavern with his normal shirt on. He has his green jacket on top of it in the next shot.

Like Father, Like Klown
When Krusty leaves the Simpsons' house, he is suddenly wearing his coat.

During dinner, Krusty does not have a shirt pocket until he pulls out his handkerchief.

Radio Bart
At the start of the scene where Bart talks to Rod and Todd on the radio, their shirt colours switch.

Separate Vocations

After Bart finds out that Lisa took the teacher's books, his Hall Monitor sash disappears and reappears for several shots.

When Lou and Eddie (the police officers) arrive at the house to take Bart for a drive, their badges are white. When they are driving in the cop car, their badges are yellow.

Tree House of Horror II: A Simpsons Halloween

Maggie gets her new pacifier and puts it in her mouth. She has her normal pacifier for the rest of this part.

Marge Gets a Job

Willie rips off his entire shirt before he fights the wolf but, in the next scene, when he is wrestling the wolf, he is wearing a torn-up shirt.

Lady Bouvier's Lover

The skin of the person who delivers the animation cell changes from white to brown and then back to white. When Bart looks through the letterbox to see who is there, his skin is white. When he gives the box to Bart, it is brown. When he hits Bart in the face and says 'that's for keeping me waiting', it is white again.

Who Shot Mr Burns? (1)

In the scene where Smithers and Mr Burns are eating the chocolate and see the photo, Marge's necklace changes from red to white and then back to red.

Homerpalooza

Homer is on stage in Springfield wearing shorts. When he jumps off the stage after dodging the cannon ball, he's wearing trousers.

King-Size Homer
Homer is stuck in the hole after saving the plant and Marge is seen in the background wearing lipstick. Mr Burns asks if there is anything he can do for them and there is a close-up of Marge and her lipstick is gone. When they cut back to Homer, Marge is again wearing lipstick.

Lisa the Iconoclast
When Lisa first discovers Jebadiah's confession, she is holding the fife and wearing his racoon hat, the screen fades to black (for the ad break) but when it comes back Lisa is standing in exactly the same position, still reading the confession, still holding the fife, but no longer wearing the hat.

The Springfield Files
After the scene with the T-shirts, when the alien arrives, Marge's 'Homer is a dope' shirt disappears and she has her normal dress on.

Alone Again Natura-Diddly
Homer's watch disappears when he is getting his car fixed.

Simpson Safari
The Simpsons, who are on the raft going down the river in Africa, come to a fork and have a choice of going to the left, towards a sunny and nicer area, or to the right where it is rainy and gloomy. As Homer tries to steer the raft to the left he pulls his left arm out of the water and it is covered in leeches but when we see the arm in the next shot of him, the leeches are gone.

The Great Money Caper
As she is driving home Marge starts to moan at the children to quieten down. In this shot she has no lipstick. In the next shot

from outside the car she has lipstick on and has it on for the rest of the scene.

I Am Furious Yellow
At the end, in the hospital, Maggie's bow is red for a second, then it changes to blue.

Papa's Got a Brand New Badge
When the family is sitting on the couch and trying to catch a breeze from the fan, Lisa's shoes disappear between shots.

Moe Baby Blues
At the birthday party Maggie is playing in the sandbox with one of Apu's sons. She and Apu's son have party hats on which are pink with green polka-dots. After she is taken out of the sandbox by Moe, Homer takes her and she keeps squirming out of his arms. Her party hat has disappeared, and never comes back.

Diatribe of a Mad Housewife
At the book signing, Dr Marvin Monroe is significantly slimmer when seen from behind than when seen from the front.

The Fat and the Furriest
When Homer realises that the bear was only aggressive because of the electrical tag, they share a bear hug. The back of Homer's shirt is torn to tatters, and his back is bleeding. Immediately after, the back of Homer's shirt is completely intact.

Sopranos, The

Another Toothpick
In the scene where Bacala is telling Uncle Jun about his father

and the accident, Uncle Junior, who is wearing glasses, gets angry and starts throwing things around. It can be seen that after throwing one of the items, he is not wearing his glasses, then he is wearing them again.

South Park

Cartman Gets an Anal Probe
Cartman is wearing gloves when he gets home from school and tells his mom about his day and about the kids calling him fat. When he sits on the couch, he has no gloves on.

Proper Condom Use
Mr Mackey's glasses do not have the part that goes over his nose unless he is looking sideways, when it suddenly appears.

Star Trek: The Next Generation

Yesterday's Enterprise
Watch the final scene with Geordi and Guinan in Ten-Forward. Although time and the universe has returned to normal, Geordi is still wearing the uniform from the alternate timeline (note the sleeve detail, and the extended neck piece).

Stargate SG-1

Tin Man
While the two Jacks are talking to each other right at the end, the camera cuts back and forth from looking over each of their shoulders at the other one. Look closely, and you will see that the false Jack's earlobe structure changes when we see him from behind.

That '70s Show

Sunday, Bloody Sunday

Kitty goes into the basement and asks for a cigarette, but the sleeve of the person that hands her one does not match that of any of the characters there.

West Wing, The

Mandatory Minimums

Toby is walking back to his office from the press room with his ex-wife whose tag and chain keeps changing through the entire sequence. Sometimes it's over her jacket with the tag just hanging, or it's under the jacket with the tag sitting just inside her jacket.

Will & Grace

Will Works Out

Karen is lying on the table with her jacket unbuttoned. When Jack pushes her off the table and she gets up, it's still unbuttoned. But as the shot cuts to her heading quickly over to the door, her jacket is buttoned, but there was no time for her to do it.

DAYLIGHT ROBBERY

Much like clothing and food, sunlight is very unforgiving to the average director. But even when you try and compensate for it, day, night, and where shadows end up isn't always under your control . . .

24

6:00 P.M.–7:00 P.M.

The 6.00 p.m.–7.00 p.m. episode ends when it is still light outside. Thc 7.00 p.m.–8.00 p.m. episode begins when it is completely dark (no sunset, dusk or twilight). The show is supposed to be in real time, but as the sun goes down it gradually gets darker, it does not just become dark from one second to the next. As it happened across an episode change they probably thought no one would notice.

Buffy the Vampire Slayer

Innocence (2)

The Scoobies are in the library and Oz says for the crew to meet outside Xander's house half an hour later. We then cut to Buffy strolling through Sunnydale High in broad daylight, then back to Oz's van outside the military base and it's the previous night again.

Intervention

When Anya and Xander see Spike and the robot in the graveyard it is night time. Xander goes back to speak to Spike almost immediately and sees Glory's followers kidnapping him. He wakes, goes back to Buffy's house and from there, again almost immediately, they go looking for Glory's house – and it is the broadest of broad daylight. It was evident that it was still night, before they left, through the windows of the house. It also begs the question of how they got Spike from Glory's house back to his crypt in the sunlight since they had no blanket and, as we all know, vampires can't go out in sunlight.

Charmed

Deja Vu All Over Again

Tempest tells Rodriguez he has brought him back to the exact moment they met. Tempest first appeared to Rodriguez at midnight, but it's light outside when he says this.

Friends

The One with the Mugging

When Phoebe and Ross are 'mugged' by Phoebe's friend it is evening and dark. However, when Ross tells Monica what has 'just' happened you can see that it is the middle of the day.

M*A*S*H

Dear Dad

When you see the shadow of the helicopter on the ground, there is no shadow of Hawkeye who is supposedly standing in the door getting ready to be lowered to the ground.

Hot Lips and Empty Arms

Margaret is drinking all of Henry's booze and it is daylight outside. Radar brings news of incoming casualties so they rush outside where it is pitch-dark.

Mail Call

When the mail arrives in the compound, in daylight, everyone has three shadows, caused by the lights used during filming.

Mr Bean

Mr Bean Goes to Town

Mr Bean arrives with his new TV and the room is dark, so he has to switch on the light. However, when he starts undressing, and goes to close the curtains, it's daylight outside: so the room should have been light when he arrived.

Only Fools and Horses

Three Men, a Woman and a Baby

Albert and Rodney are waiting in the hospital corridor; at one point it is around 2 a.m. But a view out the window and reflections show that it is broad daylight.

Simpsons, The

The Otto Show

Near the end of the episode, when Skinner shouts at Ralph to shut up, the sky outside the bus changes from night-time to daytime between shots.

A Star is Burns

When Wolfcastle says about himself that 'Jay Sherman insulted him, now he will die',, for a few shots the shadows are on the floor before they magically disappear. Also, the shadow of the gun does not match the real gun.

This Little Wiggy

In the scene in Ralph's bedroom the night-light changes positions between shots. First it's far away from the doorway, then near to it, then right next to it.

When Bart and Ralph are in the prison and see the key, the window's shadow is of four squared panels. When they go to pick the key up and the rat takes it the shadow shows three rectangular panels.

South Park

Raisins

When Kyle is lying in bed, in some shots one side of his face is in shadow; in others the opposite side is in shadow.

WHAT WAS THAT YOU WERE DOING?

Often scenes need to be cut drastically or have their audio dubbed over to make them work properly. It's a necessity for almost every production, and while it can't be avoided, the negative side effects aren't always that obvious, except once you know what to look for . . .

24

2:00 A.M.–3:00 A.M.

At about 2.15 a.m., when Jack is talking to Nina about the passenger list on the plane, we see a shot of Jack in the top left of the screen, and Nina in the top right. Because it's real time they're both meant to match up – we're watching them both at the same time. In each shot we can see the back of the other's head, but while Jack is looking down and around in the left-hand shot, in the right-hand shot his head is staying perfectly still.

5:00 A.M.–6:00 A.M.

During Season One, Jack answers his mobile to Gains and we see footage of Jack on a CCTV camera. The CCTV footage shows medical staff moving, yet when they cut back to the camera in the hall the medical staff are in different places, and they keep changing places and keep disappearing and reappearing and the CCTV footage is about two seconds ahead of the footage in the corridor.

Day 2: 12:00 Midnight–1:00 A.M.

Right at the start of the episode, Kim Bauer is seen in the liquor store being held by the neck from behind by the gun-totting Garcia as the police are closing in. In the next scene she is on the floor holding a piece of cloth against the store owner's belly wound. For a real time show that's a bit of an event gap . . .

Day 2: 2:00 P.M.–3:00 P.M.

When the police officer discovers Carla's body in Gary's car, he calls for backup just before the episode ends. At the beginning of the next episode, a minute later, at least two other police cars are there. Backup can't get there that quickly.

Alias

A Broken Heart

As Anna approaches Syd in the middle of the field, she reaches her hands up to her belt. In the very next shot from behind her, her arms are by her sides.

Angel

Hell Bound

In the scene where Spike takes the elevator to the basement, he is walking down the spooky corridor. He is supposed to be non-corporeal, so his shoes shouldn't make any sound as he walks, but you can hear his footsteps.

Black Adder

All of Series 2

The episode 'Bells' and the episode 'Head' appear to be inverted in their order. Lord Percy has a beard at the beginning of 'Bells', and shaves it off. However, in 'Head', he's got it back. In all of the other episodes, he has no beard. Also, the song at the end of 'Head' mentions Lord Blackadder's origins (it mentions Edmund's great-grandfather), which makes it more a follow-on from the first series, despite being the second episode in this series.

Buffy the Vampire Slayer

Surprise (1)
Buffy and Angel escape from Spike, Dru and the Judge and jump down into the sewer. That is fine, except that they run all of five metres and then go up the ladder to escape. However, when they come out of the sewer they are in a very open area with the factory nowhere in sight. They have not travelled far enough for this to be the case.

Anne
When the latest people to be brought into hell are lined up with a demon talking to them, there are three or four of them standing between Buffy and Lily. When the demon asks them all in turn, 'Who are you?' he is seen asking Lily and after that the shot rests on Buffy, but in the background he is heard to ask only one more person before he gets to Buffy.

Once More, With Feeling
While Anya sings her first few lines of the song 'I'll Never Tell', you can still hear Xander talking about omelettes in the background, but for the last few lines he speaks (from 'I could do an omelette' onwards) you can see over her shoulder and tell that his voice is dubbed.

Tabula Rasa
At the start of the episode the loan shark's henchmen throw a

stake at Spike and it flies over his head and hits a tree. But, a comparison of the angle from which they approach, with the relative positions of Spike and the tree, shows it would have had to do a 90-degree turn in midair to fly over his head before hitting the tree.

Empty Places

When Xander is returning from hospital, Kennedy is standing beside the couch to greet him and Willow. When Xander sits down she is sitting on the couch, but she wasn't out of shot long enough to have got there.

Get It Done

At the end of the fight with the exchange demon there is a shot of Robin helping Anya up off the ground, but Anya wasn't knocked over during the fight.

Fawlty Towers

A Touch of Class

Throughout the episode the picture Basil is distracted from putting up has no glass covering on it. However, when he smashes it at the end you can hear the distinct sound of breaking glass.

Friends

The One with the Monkey

Just after Chandler explains to Janice that, though he invited her to the party they're not going out again, she goes off crying, and Ross takes a photo. The flash is much brighter than it should be – the screen becomes a white out to disguise a jump cut – after the flash Chandler's noticeably further back than he was before.

The One with the Tiny T-Shirt
At the start when Joey comes into Monica's apartment and does his little dance number, watch his mouth as he makes his way out; it's totally out of sync with what he is saying.

The One with Rachel's Crush
In the scene where Rachel walks into the guy's new apartment and they start talking about Joshua, there's a cut to a shot of her in profile as she says 'It's just so frustrating'. Her mouth doesn't move as she says the words.

Futurama

My Problem with Popplers
Leela licks each of her four fingers once only but the sound of licking a finger plays five times.

Hollyoaks

In the episode aired on 2 January 2004 – Cameron shouted 'Don't you want a lift?' out of the car when his friends ran away (they were thinking it was a killer that had stolen the car). His lips moved when he spoke, but it was obviously a dub as the words didn't match.

M*A*S*H

The Abduction of Margaret Houlihan
When Col. Flagg makes everybody close their eyes when he

leaves, you hear the sound of glass shattering, but the window was a thick sheet of plastic.

Monty Python's Flying Circus

The Royal Philharmonic Orchestra Goes to the Bathroom
William Knickers' letter, complaining about the sketches, starts 'I strongly object . . .' but the voice-over says 'I object strongly . . .'

Only Fools and Horses

Friday the 14th
When Del, Rodney and Granddad are in the cottage, Del is scared to open the door. Rodney says 'Well go on then Del, there's nothing to be frightened of now.' There is a shot from behind Rodney when he begins to say this. Look closely at Rodney's mouth when he starts to speak; his lips aren't moving.

Red Dwarf

The End
In the 'remastered' version of this episode, when Lister and Rimmer see Cat just after Holly explains how he evolved, Rimmer runs at Cat screaming before he passes through him and we hear a crash off screen to indicate Rimmer has just run into something. He is a hologram and is not solid, so no sound should be heard.

Simpsons, The

Brush with Greatness
After the doughnut delivery guy asks Carl why all the doughnuts are piling up, Carl responds with Lenny's voice.

Bart the Murderer
When Bart arrives late at the social club, he is mumbling. His mouth doesn't move.

Homer Defined
After Barney falls over in his chair, you can hear him say, 'Hmm, a pretzel.' His mouth doesn't move.

I Married Marge
Marge sees the letter from Homer and says, 'You won't see me again until I'm a man.' On the paper though, it reads, 'But you will not see me–' and the sentence is cut off; the rest of the paper is blank.

Lisa's Pony
As Lisa rides past on her pony, Ralph is sitting on the fence with another boy who says, 'She really tamed that horse', Ralph says, 'Yes, but who can tame her?' For some bizarre reason he speaks in Nelson's voice.

Homer's Barbershop Quartet
The Bee Sharps are singing 'Goodbye my Coney Island Baby' next to the Statue of Liberty and Chief Wiggum's voice is heard singing with the other members of the group – but he got chucked out of the group earlier on in the episode.

The Two Mrs Nahasapeemapetilons
When Homer is running for the food, after racing in the wheel-chair with Jasper, he says, 'Eat my dust', but his lips don't move for the 'my dust' part.

The Old Man and the C Student
Homer flushes his springs one by one and sings a parody of 'Ten

Green Bottles', but with flushing springs. He goes from 999 to 996 but doesn't flush the toilet enough times to get to that number.

Skinner's Sense of Snow

While Principal Skinner is watching the kids throw the books in the fire, someone starts to throw *Huckleberry Finn*, or a book like that into the fire. He starts to say something like, 'it took me hours to. . .', and while he says this his lips are out of sync with the words.

THINGS THAT MOVE BETWEEN TAKES

I realise this is a horribly vague category, but when all is said and done there's a whole load of mistakes that just fall into a general 'that wasn't meant to happen' group . . .

24

Day 2: 12:00 Midnight–1:00 A.M.
As Kate and Jack are escaping CTU the security guard tries to close the gate and the wingmirror breaks off one of the car doors. Later on both of the mirrors are seen back on the car in one piece.

When Yousef uses his Nextel to call Jack he uses the direct connect button (which makes it act like a walkie-talkie). This means that only one person can talk at a time with a noise identifying the change from one to the other. Yet when Jack gives the phone to Wallace it is a regular call, not a direct connect – these noises are missing.

Day 2: 5:00 P.M.–6:00 P.M.
Marie Warner goes to see Reza at her father's office at about 5.30. When she enters the office, she puts her handbag on the table and embraces Reza. After they embrace she picks up her handbag from the floor next to Reza's chair. There was no time or opportunity for anyone to move her bag.

Day 2: 7:00 A.M.–8:00 A.M.
Palmer's attorney tells Mike that he found a record of phone

calls from Peter Kingsley to Jonathan Wallace, as recently as six hours ago. This means that the last call would have been made at about 1.04 a.m., just as Wallace was in a major shoot-out and had no way to talk on the phone.

Alias

Phase One

During the day Sydney tells Will to 'Get Francie and get out of town' because she realises there's someone after her. Later that night Francie is shot at her restaurant and replaced by Allison (the clone), but Will was supposed to have taken her away already. There's no question of him not finding her – the restaurant would be the first place he'd look for her.

The Abduction

Sydney shuts down the traffic lights while Sark's car is in the middle of the gridlock. When Sydney is fleeing with the stolen briefcase seconds later Sark pulls up beside her to save her, but he was jammed in traffic – how did he get out of the huge grid-lock?

Ally McBeal

Silver Bells

In the first episode, Richard Fish invites Ally to join his law firm, saying that he has only recently set it up, yet in the Christmas episode of Season One, Elaine says that singing at the party is an annual tradition in the firm and also that they have had at least three Christmas parties. That much time has not passed since Ally joined.

Angel

Five By Five
Faith breaks down and cries at the end of the episode and Wesley is seen to drop his knife; it falls in slow-motion at his feet. However, in the final long shot right before the credits the knife is nowhere to be seen.

All of Season Two
In the Season Three episode 'Anne' of *Buffy the Vampire Slayer*, the character 'Anne', who later appears on *Angel* running a youth shelter, had a rather large red tattoo of half a heart on her arm. However, no trace of it is to be found when she is on *Angel*. Tattoo removal is a rather pricey procedure, and she seems to be tight on cash until she gets the two million from Wolfram and Hart. Even if Wolfram and Hart would have paid for the procedure, there would be some scarring or residual pigments for such a large tattoo. It's definitely the same character – Anne says that she used to think vampires were cool, until she met one. That's a reference to her first appearance (as 'Chanterelle' in *Buffy*), in which she belonged to a vampire-loving cult.

Players
Gwen is struck by lightning and we later see that the envelope she was holding is badly scorched. The papers that were inside, however, don't have a mark on them. Unless that was an asbestos envelope it doesn't make much sense.

Are You Being Served?

Across whole show
The Gentlemen's and Ladies' Department is on the first, third, or

fourth floor of Grace Brothers, depending on the episode, presumably to meet the different needs of the plot.

Band of Brothers

Carentan

During the first battle in the city, watch the part where two soldiers go in the house with the backyard shed (right before the same house gets bombed). Paranoid, one of the two soldiers shoots the backyard shed twice over a period of about five seconds. In his first shot, one bullet hole appears. In his second shot, two bullet holes appear. How can one bullet make two holes?

In the scene where Capt. Winters is telling Blithe to shoot his M1 Garand, he starts and shoots eight rounds in the slow-motion part. The clip should be empty and the Garand should ping as it ejects the empty clip, but Blithe shoots four more bullets (making twelve shots total). An M1 Garand only holds eight rounds, so where on earth did he get the extra four?

Crossroads

When they are assaulting the German companies, Winters is in the lead and Arter puts a round in the first German. The rifle he's using holds a seven-round clip, but he shoots off nine more (two too many shots), then reloads and only shoots six off (two too few). In both cases the clip ejects as if fully used.

Why We Fight

Capt. Nixon is running out of booze while he is playing poker with some other officers and he goes out to take a walk. After a while he stops in front of a shop window and smashes a petrol can from a nearby jeep through the glass. There is a big hole in the window, but it's not big enough for him to get through. Two shots later there is no glass at all in the shop window, even though he never had the time to remove the rest of it.

Black Adder

All of Series Two

During the introduction, the snake tries to get away from Blackadder. He gets the snake. Its head is above a black tile. There is then a close-up of the snake, and Blackadder wags his finger at it. It is now above a white tile.

Beer

Blackadder, Queenie and Nursey are all comforting Melchett. There is a shot of Melchett from the side view, where he is holding his head with his left hand. Then there is a shot from behind Melchett, where he still has his hand on his head, but when the shot returns to the side, Melchett now no longer has his hand on his head.

Chains

At the very end of the episode, to the right of all the dead bodies, 'Queenie' (actually the impostor) can be seen for a few seconds. The dagger she is holding is pointing upwards. Then there is a close-up of Queenie, who talks to the audience in Prince Ludwig's voice, and the dagger she is holding is now pointing downwards.

Bottom

Culture

After Eddie has performed checkmate on Richie, Richie punches Eddie, who falls over. Eddie gets up and lifts the table up. The chess board, ashtray, bottle of brown sauce and other things on the table have disappeared completely in the next shot which shows the table landing on Richie's feet.

Holy

Eddie and Richie are by the table discussing the eight quid Eddie spent on the brandy and there is a shot of the table with no Christmas tree on it. But during the next few close-ups and then another wide angle shot, a Christmas tree apparently materialises from nowhere.

Boy Meets World

Across whole show

When the house is shown from the front, there is a window on the left, but inside there is a hat rack there, and no window.

Notorious

In this episode, Mr Feeny's office is across from Mr Turner's class. But in other episodes, the room used as his office is the boys' toilets.

Class Pre-Union

The sign at the class reunion says 'Welcome Back, Class of 2000', but the characters actually graduated from high school in a 1998 episode.

Cory's Alternative Friends

Mr Feeny says he taught sixth grade for many years, but later in the series it is established (against all educational practice) that he has been Cory and Shawn's teacher for every single year of their lives.

Shawn claims his 'sister, Stacey' uses the hair-straightening stuff all the time. This is the only mention of her ever during the entire run of the show; but when Jack joins the show he is established as Shawn's only sibling. What happened to his sister?

Band on the Run

Cory and Shawn are auditioning for 'Guys' and they're talking about the first person they pick. Cory says, 'He's shorter than me and . . .' But after they pick two guys and he's talking to them, you can see that Cory is actually the shorter one.

Pop Quiz

Cory and Shawn, who are on Cory's bed, throw a ball out of the window. But when the camera focuses on them again you can see that that ball is on Eric's bed. But just a second later the ball has disappeared.

This Little Piggy

Turner goes into a room and says it's his bedroom. But in 'My Best Friend's Girl' Cory goes into that room and they say it's a closet. Some major house redesigning going on there . . .

In this episode, Little Cory is a small pink pig. In a later episode, Little Cory is shown again, but he is now a fat black pig.

Singled Out

When Eric answers one question on MTV's dating show *Singled Out*, almost the entire group of girls leaves. In the next scene they have reappeared and the stage is suddenly filled again.

They're Killing Us
The firefighters, apparently the fastest men in the universe, appear no more than ten seconds after the fire starts.

Buffy the Vampire Slayer

Angel
During the climax at the Bronze Buffy puts down her crossbow and walks towards Angel for about five steps. When Darla bursts in a few seconds later the crossbow is back at her feet, but it should be a few feet behind her.

I Robot, You Jane
How exactly does Willow scan Moloch out of his book when the scan she does is only about two-thirds the width of the book? She only does one pass.

Prophecy Girl
Buffy drowns after she falls into the pool with her hair tied in a ponytail and her arms under her. When she is discovered by Angel and Xander, her arms are by her sides and her hair is loose. That's a lot of moving for a drowned woman.

Teacher's Pet
Buffy finds Dr Gregory's glasses on the lab floor and places them on the table. From the long shot she places them at the left end of the table near a plastic tub with a white lid, with the glasses open. Then a cut to a close-up shows them in front of a book on the right side of the table and they are closed. A further cut to a long shot and they are back in the original place.

The Harvest (2)
Cordelia tells Buffy there's no cover charge to get into the Bronze but, later in the episode, right before the vampires attack the Bronze, the bouncer is taking money from people on their way in.

On the night of the Harvest, Cordelia says that she is going to the Bronze – it's a Friday. Strangely enough, everyone seems to be back at school the next day, which would be Saturday.

Becoming Part 1
Drusilla kills Kendra by cutting open her jugular artery and leaving her to bleed to death. Buffy turns up a while later but there is not a drop of blood to be seen anywhere.

Inca Mummy Girl
When Xander and Ampata are attacked by the bodyguard on the bleachers, Xander's bag is knocked over and then rolls down about four rows. Seconds later, when they stand up to run away, the bag is right beside his feet again.

School Hard
While studying at the Bronze, Buffy and Willow go and dance leaving their books spread out all over the table. Spike calls them outside to fight a vampire and, when Xander runs back inside to grab a stake, the books have all been put back into Buffy's bag.

Some Assembly Required
Eric takes photos of Cordelia and Buffy. Later, when he's developing them, the poses in the photos are different from the way the girls were standing at the time.

What's My Line? (1)
If Spike and his gang take only a few hours to break through the door to Ford's club in 'Lie To Me' (which we are told is six feet of solid steel), why can't Angel, given the same amount of time, break through a thin wire door that visibly shakes every time he hits it? Angel and Spike are as strong as each other, in fact Angel's probably stronger.

Buffy is fighting Kendra, but the fragments of the table that broke when she was thrown onto it have disappeared when she stands up again. Most obviously missing is the large chunk that was under her right arm.

In this episode, Spike says the ritual to restore Drusilla's health must be done on the night of a full moon, but in 'What's My Line?' Part 2 Giles says the ritual will take place on the night of a new moon.

Amends
During Season Seven we are told several times that The First cannot take corporeal form, i.e. it cannot touch things. However, in its first appearance in the Season Three episode 'Amends', when it manifests as Jenny Calender and runs its fingers through Angel's hair, you can see his hair moving underneath her fingers. This should be impossible.

Consequences
Buffy says to Faith, 'Less than twenty-four hours ago you killed a man'. However, in 'Bad Girls', Faith kills Finch in the alley on the first night. One night later Buffy and Angel are attacking Belthazor, and the next night Buffy dreams about drowning, so Buffy's assertion is actually about 72 hours after the murder.

Earshot

When everyone is in the library and they find out that Buffy can hear thoughts, Buffy turns to look at Wesley because he is thinking about Cordelia. As she leans forward she rests her chin on the heel of her hand, the shot cuts to Wesley, then back to Buffy and she has her chin resting on the top of her hand (the knuckles). Wesley then goes into the office and a cut to a shot of Buffy and Willow shows Buffy is once again resting her chin on the heel of her hands.

Graduation Day (1)

Faith and Buffy are fighting; Faith throws Buffy into the wall near the TV – the TV is left intact. A few shots later, there is debris on the floor, glass and such, from the previously unbroken TV, but when it's shown again, the TV is still unbroken. This happens a few times. In 'Graduation Day' Part 2, when Faith and Buffy are talking in the apartment, the TV is broken again.

Graduation Day (2)

Percy and some guys, who are presumably other students, are fighting at Angel's side, but shouldn't they have been at the ceremony with the others? Even if they just didn't show up there would have been noticeable gaps in the seating, but in all the previous shots every chair is filled.

The Wish

When Cordelia is cutting up the photo of Xander at the start of this episode she chops his head off high up on the neck. When she sets fire to the remains it shows a piece of the photo burning, and the cut is now around shoulder level.

A New Man

In the scene where Giles and Ethan Rayne are drinking in the bar, the shots cut between Giles and Ethan frequently. When focusing on Giles, you can see Ethan's hands and arms, and his glass in the foreground of the shot, but almost every time the shot switches back to Ethan he's in a different position with no time to have moved.

The I in Team

In every other episode it's seen in, room 314 is a room directly off a corridor, but in this episode Walsh walks through the door off the corridor, then there's another shot of her walking through another door. Where did the second door come from?

The Initiative

Riley is looking for Spike with a heat-sensitive camera and says, 'We've got a cold one.' If Spike was at room temperature as indicated on the sensor, he would be indistinguishable from the air and objects in the room. Vampires are never shown as being colder than the air around them.

Riley, Graham and Forrest, wearing thermal goggles, are looking in through the windows of Stevenson Hall searching for Spike. They see him walking towards Willow. When we cut to an inside shot seconds later and see Willow and Spike, he is still sitting on the bed where he has been for most of the scene.

This Year's Girl (1)

Faith, who is taunting Joyce with all Buffy's uncollected mail, flings the envelopes across the bed one by one, scattering them. When Faith is fighting Buffy later on they are all in a nice neat pile again.

I Was Made to Love You

Warren has just finished packing his bags and is about to run out of the door when Buffy arrives. Later, Spike shows up at his house and he's still packing his bags, despite having finished earlier on.

Real Me

When Buffy is fighting Mort in Harmony's lair, she knocks him up against the wall in a flurry of blows. In the next shot, he is several steps away from the wall and facing in a different direction.

All the Way

A vampire kicks through a car window trying to hit Buffy and some shards of glass are still standing in the window frame. The angle changes, and the shards are gone.

Bargaining (1)

Anya is talking to Giles while he trains the Buffybot. There's a shot from behind and the corner of her jumper moves around as she turns away, then it cuts back to a front view of her and she's still facing Giles.

Flooded

Jonathan reads a few things off the board listing the Trio's ultimate aims. One of the things he reads out is 'prototype jet-packs that actually fly', but when the list is shown a few seconds later jet-packs aren't mentioned on it.

Life Serial

Warren, who is in the college corridor looking up at the camera, has loads of students around him, but when we see things on

Jonathan and Andrew's monitors, the corridor around him is deserted.

Once More, with Feeling

The demons that Buffy fights and conquers change positions on the floor during the following song.

During the episode 'All The Way' Anya mentions that she's having a huge blowout sale the next day. The next episode is this one, which picks up the very next morning (Tara wakes up to find the Lethe's bramble on her pillow, which Willow placed there at the end of 'All The Way'), but during the scenes in the shop on that day there are no signs, no banners, no customers – nothing to indicate a huge sale.

Buffy is singing 'Something to Sing About', and when she sings the verse beginning 'All the joy life sends, family and friends', we see that Anya and Tara are standing in the background, about three metres apart from each other. However, for just one shot they're much closer together.

Tabula Rasa

When they all – Buffy, Xander, Willow, Tara, Dawn, Spike, Giles and Anya – collapse in The Magic Box, Spike is kind of slumped over on the counter but then, in the next shot, he's lying comfortably on his back with his arms crossed behind his head.

Buffy and the gang are fighting the vampires on the front lawn of a house. Buffy breaks the pole off of a mailbox and uses it to stake a vampire. In the shot where she breaks it off the ends are uneven but, in the very next shot, one end has a point like a stake.

Chosen

Sunnydale apparently has docks (seen in 'Consequences' and 'Surprise') and is quite close to a beach ('Go Fish'), but when Sunnydale is destroyed in this episode, we see an overhead shot of the crater and it appears to be in the middle of the desert, far from any coastline.

In the shot right before Spike's amulet sends out the blast through the roof, you can see an ubervamp just about to pin him against the wall, and in the next shot he is standing in the middle of the area backing up towards the stairs. He then sends out the blast. There would never be enough time between the shots for Spike to break free before going to stand in the middle of the floor.

Him

Any girl who sees RJ wearing his jacket falls in love with him. However, when Buffy, Willow and Xander are in the Bronze watching Dawn dance with RJ, he is wearing his magic jacket but Buffy and Willow don't fall under the spell until they see him again later on in the episode.

Touched

Spike tells Buffy that her theory about the vineyard was right, but he wasn't there when she suggested this theory (in the episode 'Empty Places'), and no one from the group that did hear it told him about it.

Charmed

Out of Sight

Prue is pouring a potion into jars when the phone rings. When she sets the pot down there is one full jar and one empty jar; when she runs back a few seconds later to grab the potion both jars are full.

Sam I Am
When Paige and Phoebe are sitting at the bar at the beginning of the episode, their arms change positions between every shot.

The Eyes Have It
Lydia has green eyes, but when Orin extracts them at the morgue, the eyes he puts into his head are blue.

The Importance of Being Phoebe
When Kaya throws the knife at Phoebe, if you watch in freeze-frame you can see that, for the shot from behind Kaya, there's no knife in her hands.

Coronation Street

Across whole show
Martin's car was parked outside on the episode first broadcast on 15 December 2003. It wasn't used at all in the day, but at night when he came to use it, it had moved position outside his house.

CSI: Crime Scene Investigation

Feeling the Heat
The baby's car seat goes from front-facing when they find him to rear-facing and still strapped in when they go to investigate the car. Also, a baby that young would be in a rear-facing car seat anyway.

Dawson's Creek

All Good Things . . . (1)

Joey is kissing Chris at the start of the episode and at first her hand is down, resting on the cushion. When the shot changes (right before she asks, 'I don't really sound like her, do I?') her hand is up on the back of his neck.

ER

Now What?

The first scene shows a family climbing into a gold Volvo 240 estate car, a woman driving and children in the back. In the following crash scene involving the same family, where the car flips and is impaled by a truck, the car is a gold Volvo 740 estate.

Family Guy

Death Has a Shadow

Brian's newspaper's name changes from *Daily Informant* to *Daily Tim . . .*

Peter and Brian are talking after Peter called Lois fat and underneath Brian's hand is a rolled up *Daily Times*. In the next shot, the newspaper has turned upside down.

Dammit Janet

When Stewie is building with blocks, you first see a pyramid with three blocks on the bottom and two on the top. The shot changes, and he puts two more on the top, near the edge. A further change of shot shows there are five blocks on the bottom, six on the second layer and two on the top near the middle. The letters and pictures are also different.

Death Is a Bitch

Peter enters the cockpit and accidentally kills the pilots. The cockpit looks only big enough to fit Peter and the pilots in their seats. However, when he turns around to leave, the cockpit looks big enough to fit a sizeable group of people.

A Fish Out of Water

Lois and Meg take the red car for their vacation at the spa, but while they are gone, Peter is seen driving it on a number of occasions.

And the Wiener is . . .

When the flag team first walks out to the field, they are all in a straight line. Next time they are in two separate lines with Meg at the head. There is not enough time for them to move into the lines. Also, the girl with the head brace has moved to the front after being seen in the back.

From Method to Madness

In Stewie's first acting class, the chairs the children are sitting on are blue, but after Stewie has finished his scene and he is talking to Olivia about her comment, the chairs are orange.

Mr Saturday Knight

During the 'So Long, Farewell' parody, Stewie is seen putting his head on the stairs' landing; when it cuts back to him, his head is resting on the second stair from the top.

The Kiss Seen Around the World

When Stewie has kidnapped the bully he holds a weapon in front of the bully's face. When Lois comes in he puts it down, but in a full shot of the room it has disappeared.

Father Ted

Night of the Nearly Dead

In the scene where the old women are grabbing at Eoin at the front door, the top pane of the window on the left of the door is broken, in one shot, and an arm is coming through it; in another shot the bottom pane is broken and the top one is intact and the arm is coming through the bottom pane. In the very next shot the top pane is again broken and the bottom one is intact.

Fawlty Towers

Gourmet Night

When Manuel goes outside to fetch Basil, Basil enters the building first in the exterior shots, yet Manuel gets to reception first in the interior ones.

The Psychiatrist

There are distinct disparities between the locations of rooms and the windows on the outside of the hotel. This is particularly noticeable in this episode when Basil climbs a ladder to look through the window.

In this episode, Basil hides in a cupboard to try and trap a girl staying the night in a guest's room. However, in other episodes ('Wedding Guests', 'Communication Problems', and 'The Kipper and the Corpse'), there is a room in the same spot as the cupboard in this episode.

Frasier

Three Dates and a Breakup (2)

While Marty and Frasier are fighting, Marty smashes some plates. The shot changes to the living room, with Frasier apologising, and then switches back again. However, all the smashed crockery has disappeared to be replaced by what appears to be a bowl and a tumbler.

Lilith Needs a Favour

In one shot Niles is on the phone to Daphne, in the next he's already hung up the phone and put it away, without as much as a 'goodbye'.

Friends

All of Season One

The number of the flats after the start of the first season was four and five. A few shows later they changed to nineteen and twenty. The producers realised that the numbers four and five were for apartments on the lower floors and had shown Monica's apartment to be much higher up in fill-in shots, so they changed the numbers – that's the reason but it's still a mistake.

The One with the Blackout

In the scene where Joey is standing with candlelight over Ross's neck, the candle is full length, but in the next shot the candle is only half length.

The One with the Dozen Lasagnes
Rachel talks with Phoebe about Paolo. In this scene Rachel rolls off some kitchen-paper and uses it as a tissue. Initially she's holding two torn halves attached to the roll, then, when she says 'he's a pig', it goes to a whole sheet not attached to any others, but when she sits down it's a whole sheet attached to the roll again. Also, when Phoebe sits, in some shots the paper is on the table, in others it's not.

The One with the Monkey
Max tells the gang that he and David are going to Minsk. Phoebe asks, incredulously, 'Minsk?' and Max replies 'Yes, Minsk. It's in Russia.' Minsk is not in Russia, it's in Belarus.

The One where Dr Ramoray Dies
Joey, who gets his own apartment an episode or two earlier than this one, takes the gang on a tour of it. In the bathroom, we can clearly see the shower *door*. But, in this episode, when Monica is trying to cheer him up, she tells him that she straightened out his shower *curtain* so it wouldn't get mildew.

The One where No One's Ready
After Phoebe asks Monica what gets out houmous stains, Monica comes out of her bedroom. In the wide shot she's standing next to Ross, in the close-up he's holding her by the arm.

When Ross asks Chandler, 'you took his underwear?', the angle changes halfway through the line. Chandler's hands go from in front of him to being in his pockets.

The One with the Dollhouse
While Monica and Phoebe are looking at the Dollhouse, Monica

says, 'I don't want a ghost for the house.' When she says this, the camera is behind Phoebe whose right hand is up in the air. The shot then switches to Phoebe from the front – her hand has instantly gone to her lap.

The One with the Princess Leia Fantasy

When Joey says, 'we'll call that plan B, all right?', Monica has her chin in her hand. When there's a cut to a different angle, she's got both arms on the table. Rachel also goes from having both hands clasped under her chin to having one arm resting on the table and one reaching for coffee.

The One with All the Haste

At the beginning of the episode, Phoebe comes in wearing Santa pants. When Joey and Chandler point out that she's wearing Santa pants, Chandler's legs are crossed or uncrossed, depending on the camera angle.

The One with Joey's New Girlfriend

Chandler has fallen for Joey's girlfriend Kathy. There is a scene where he is chasing her down the street trying to get her attention. During a close-up of him running, just before the camera cuts away, we see a guy's face on the left; when it cuts back to Chandler he runs for a while and then encounters the same guy (the dog-walker). Also, when he finally lands in front of Kathy, there is a bike rider coming towards them, but as the camera cuts back and forth between the two, the rider never passes them.

The One with Rachel's New Dress

In Joshua's parents' house, Rachel is in her underwear/'new dress' on the sofa when Joshua comes in. In wide shots focusing on Joshua she's lying back slightly, but in close shots of her she's sitting more upright. Worse than that, her legs are crossed, but uncross in the shot where his parents come in, only to re-cross in the next shot when she gasps.

The One with the 'Cuffs
Joey's encounter with the encyclopedia salesman is riddled with errors. First, the salesman is talking about Van Gogh and saying 'He painted that', and points to a page that is all text; later, Joey is reading about vomit, and it is at a much further point in the book than when the salesman read about vulcanised rubber (which it shouldn't be, given that the encyclopedia is alphabetical); finally, when Joey buys the 'V' volume, and opens it, he has a $50 bill in his hand, but when the shot changes, the salesman is somehow folding and pocketing the bill without having taken it from Joey.

The One where Ross Moves In
Chandler and Joey are on their couch thinking what to do about Ross, and when Chandler says 'what are we gonna do?', he switches from crossed arms to hands folded in his lap.

At the start of the episode, when Joey is showing Chandler the *National Geographic*, Chandler has his left hand up by his face in one shot then, when the angle changes, they're both clasped in his lap.

The One with All the Kissing
Phoebe grabs a photo of the other five by the Tower of London, in frustration at Monica claiming it's of 'all of us'. When we see a shot of her a few seconds later drawing herself into the photo, it's a different photograph.

The One with All the Resolutions

Joey and Rachel, who are trying to work out if the other knows about Monica and Chandler, sit at the table in silence. In a side shot of Joey they look at each other sneakily. Joey has his arms by his sides. It then cuts to a head-on shot of Joey – he's got his right arm over the back of the chair.

When Ross first enters Elizabeth's bathroom, it can be seen that on the shelf where he gets the powder from, the lotion is first in line, then something else, then the powder. Later, it is noticeable that the powder is first in line on the shelf and the lotion is where Ross picks it up.

The One with All the Thanksgivings

At the beginning of the episode Phoebe is trying to make the TV work. In the close-ups and the first wide shot the remote is at an angle, but in the second wide shot it's straight. It then goes back to being at an angle.

The One with Ross's Sandwich

In the scene where Joey has just brought home his date, he jiggles the door handle, which makes Monica and Chandler run off into Chandler's room. Chandler kicks a circle cushion off the mat but, when the camera cuts back, it's on the mat again and then off the mat again when Rachel walks in.

The One with the Inappropriate Sister

Phoebe is complaining about people disrespecting her charity bucket and hands the bucket to Monica as she does so. In the first two shots Monica holds the bucket by its edge, but when the camera goes back to her for a third time, she is holding the bucket by its handle when she wouldn't really have had time to change to holding the handle as her other hand is already holding a glass of orange juice.

The One That Could Have Been, Part 1
Near the start of the episode, Chandler is sitting in the coffee house in the big chair. As he talks to Joey about money, his feet change positions with every shot, which seems to be about every two seconds. On the floor, crossed, resting on the table, the list goes on and on.

The One where Chandler Can't Cry
In the previous episode Monica had a very bad cold and she tried to have sex with Chandler. This episode carries on immediately after the end of the last one (Monica's still in her dressing gown from earlier), but that must have been some good sex, because Monica isn't coughing or sneezing any more.

In the scene where Chandler throws the book of *Chicken Soup for the Soul* under the sofa and it goes across the floor to Monica's feet, she kneels down to pick it up by the counter next to the door, but when she rises, she's next to a chair that's under the table.

The One where Phoebe Runs
Rachel runs into the horse at the end of the episode and there is a shot of the horse looking round at her. When the shot changes angle to show Rachel picking herself up you can see that the horse is still looking straight ahead.

The One with Rachel's Sister
When Reese drops her shopping bags on the coffee shop table, the small blue Tiffany's bag is visible on the end of the line. But it is not visible in any shots after Rachel comes in. Additionally,

when Rachel grabs the bags and leaves, Ross seems to pick the little blue bag up off the floor, though it is not shown how the bag got there.

The One with the Proposal, Part 2
Monica, who is in Richard's apartment, gets all worked up, so Richard gives her a hug to calm her down. She goes into the hug with her arms curled up in front of her face, but when the camera angle changes, they are behind Richard's back, a move she didn't have time to make.

The One with the Ring
Joey has got Chandler's credit card and when we see Joey with it in the coffee house it is a Mastercard. But when Chandler gets it from Joey in his apartment later, it's clearly an American Express card.

The One where They All Turn Thirty
Monica is at the party and she is drunk. There is one point when she is sitting down on a chair, with Chandler on her right. Chandler is holding her left hand (which has a snack in it), but when it cuts to a front view of Monica, her hands are on her lap.

The One with All the Candy
Ross is trying to convince Phoebe to try and learn to ride her bike again, which is completely covered by a large white sheet in the corner of Phoebe's room. However, in a later shot, the wheel of the bike is visible.

The One with Chandler's Dad
The number plate on the Porsche changes between the time it is seen outside the coffee shop (YSO 791) and the time Rachel and Ross are seen driving on the highway (XL 334).

The One with Rachel's Big Kiss
Melissa and Rachel are reunited at Central Perk. The way they hold their arms (crossed, hands on hips, etc.) changes with almost every shot.

The One with the Nap Partners
After Rachel shows Phoebe all the stuff she was saving for Monica's wedding, she leaves it on the couch. Monica walks in briefly and, after she leaves, all the stuff on the couch is gone too.

All of Season Eight
Chandler and Joey's pets, the chick and the duck, first appeared in Season Three and were seen regularly in the following four seasons. They simply disappear in Season Eight without any explanation.

The One where Rachel Tells . . .
Monica is sitting in the living room with all her wedding presents, waiting for Chandler to return. She begins to open a large parcel and reveals a brown cardboard box. The camera moves to Joey, and when it moves back, the parcel is wrapped up again. This happens about three times.

The One with the Baby Shower
Monica needs to ring Rachel's mum to invite her to Rachel's baby shower. She says that she has her number in her phone book and walks over to the phone – we see her start to look in it, but when the angle changes she's got the phone and is already dialling.

The One with the Birthing Video
Chandler watches the video of a woman giving birth and, after

being shocked by the tape, he's obviously taken it out of the video recorder – he's staring at the box on the table and when Monica moves it we hear that a tape's inside. When Monica asks him what he is so upset about he presses play on the remote control. The tape immediately starts playing, despite no one moving to put it in the recorder.

The One with the Rumour

When Ross and Will are standing by the fridge and Rachel comes in, Will's right hand jumps around after he crushes the decoration on the wall.

Monica begins showing Phoebe how she's meant to fold the napkins like swans. However, Phoebe manages to get out of it to 'watch the game' with Chandler You would therefore think that Monica would have folded them into swans herself, seeing as she always has to have everything perfect, but there is no sign of napkins, never mind 'swan' napkins, at the table when they have their meal.

The One in Barbados, Part 2

Just after Monica bashes her hand against the table, the shot of Chandler asking if she's OK shows Monica raising a finger right at the edge of the screen. We then cut to Monica, who's cradling both her hands together.

When Mike and Monica are playing table tennis, Mike goes to great pains to explain that if a player puts their free hand on the table while the ball is in play then the player forfeits the point. Just before Mike wins his game (the second game they play) he stretches to get a shot from Monica and places his free hand on the table.

The One with Phoebe's Birthday Dinner
Across the whole show, whenever Ross closes his apartment door, it door remains unlocked; but in this episode, when he and Rachel go outside, the door locks itself.

The One with Phoebe's Rats
As Rachel says, 'the guy hates me', Monica, in a wide shot, turns to her with her arms by her sides to say, 'does he?'. The camera then cuts to a shot more focused on Monica (where she laughs), and she's now reaching forwards to the table.

At the end of the episode when Rachel is on the balcony with Gavin, before he says, 'I do have feelings for you', in the shot from the front angle his hand is on the wall of the balcony. When the shot switches to over his shoulder his hand is suddenly by his side.

Monica goes to Rachel's office and invites Gavin to Rachel's birthday party. Rachel gets up and goes to the door exclaiming, 'Why did you invite him, I hate that guy.' She has nothing in her hand when she gets up from her desk; but at the very end of the scene when she tells Monica to be quiet, she's got a pen in her hand for one shot.

The One with the Blind Dates
At the end of the blind date, in shots of Rachel, her date Steve is holding her hand with both of his, but from the reverse angle he's only using one hand.

The One with the Lottery
Joey and Phoebe are holding the lucky bone, which they have to break and then make a wish. Look at Joey's thumb, the location of it changes between shots.

Just after Chandler has got the job and he sits down you can see Joey's hands on the right side of the screen – he unclasps them and holds them palm up in a questioning way. However, when the shot changes to a better view of Joey, his hands are relaxed, holding a bit of paper. He then holds them palm up in a questioning way again.

The One with the Male Nanny
Ross walks in on Sandy and Joey playing the recorders and Joey puts his recorder down on the table in front of him. When Ross storms out of the room, the recorder is in a totally different position on the far end of the table.

Futurama

Space Pilot 3000
Leela's chip implanter gun disappears immediately after she falls into the cryogenics chamber.

Mars University
When everyone is floating towards the waterfall, the rock that saves them appears out of nowhere.

The Honking
In one shot we see Bender become a 'were-car' and a bumper sticker on him reads, 'If you can read this, I've run you over.' But it's not there for any other shots. Also, it wasn't on Bender when he transformed, so where did it come from?

Jurassic Bark
The lava is close to the machine, until Fry runs to it, then it somehow changes to being a long way away.

The Route of All Evil
The comic book pages suddenly become blank when Cubert is ripping off the back page.

M*A*S*H

Across whole show
In the pilot episode, the MASH unit holds the raffle to send Ho Jon to medical school. In the rest of the series, Ho Jon is still at the MASH unit.

Dear Dad, Again
In some shots, Radar's exam questions are in his hand, in others they are tucked under his arm.

Germ Warfare
Radar hangs the hammer on the OUT OF ORDER sign and it is covering the 'of'. When he and Frank walk away the hammer has moved and is covering the 't'.

Henry, Please Come Home
As Henry is receiving his medal, Hawkeye walks up and stands close behind a man who is standing up, and two women who are sitting down. The camera angle switches to show Hawkeye talking to Trapper, and now they are standing behind two standing women.

Sometimes You Hear the Bullet
Frank and Margaret are dancing in her tent when Frank's back seizes up; in the subsequent shots sometimes his arms are around her waist and sometimes around her shoulders.

Hawkeye lifts Wendell's arm, takes his pulse and lays his arm down by his side again. In the next shot, Wendell's arm is across his chest.

The Ringbanger
When Radar is slipping the glass of milk into Buzz's tent, we see the outside of the tent and there are no windows. From the inside, the milk is placed on a table that is right under a window.

Iron Guts Kelly
The length of the chewing gum hanging from Henry's hat differs between the front and rear shots.

Officer of the Day
Hawkeye is in the swamp talking with Trapper. Hawkeye leaves and walks past the tent, and Trapper is no longer inside.

Payday
When the Captain from Accounting and Finance interrupts the poker game to arrest Hawkeye he leans over, puts the file down in front of Henry and asks him to sign it. In the next shot, the Captain is standing back from the table with the file under his arm.

White Gold
After Perkins is recaptured, Henry leaves his office with his cigar in his mouth. In the next shot, of him coming through the door from the other side, his cigar is in his hand.

Der Tag
Early in the episode it is stated that Margaret's tent door is padlocked while she is in Tokyo. But when she gets back, she just walks straight in without needing to unlock anything.

The Kids
While Hawkeye is examining the orphan who is wiggling his tongue, there are two camera angles: one of Hawkeye from the front and one of the orphan over Hawkeye's shoulder. In the first shot, the tongue depressor that Hawkeye is holding is horizontal, in the other it is vertical. This flips back and forth a couple of times.

Welcome to Korea (60 mins.)
When Radar and Burns leave the tent for morning parade, Radar's clipboard acquires a pencil.

Movie Tonight
While Klinger is mending the movie, the amount of film on the two reels changes a lot between shots.

The General's Practitioner
Near the beginning of this episode, while Col. Bidwell is watching Hawkeye operate, in the close-ups he is standing by the window, but in the wide shots he is standing in a different part of the OR.

Goodbye, Farewell and Amen
Early in the episode a tank is driven into the MASH compound by a wounded soldier (demolishing the latrine in the process). The tank is an M41 dating from the early 1950s – it is squat and angular in shape. Later, after the tank has been hidden under a tent, Hawkeye decides to drive the tank into the camp dump (demolishing the new latrine on the way). The tank has changed into a Sherman (World War Two era), which is a lot higher and more rounded in shape.

Malcolm in the Middle

Malcolm vs. Reese
When Francis gets pulled over, his window is open and closed between shots.

Midsomer Murders

Bad Tidings
When Helen Grace is in the retired GP's house choosing which apple she will eventually stuff into her victim's mouth, her hand wavers over one apple, but instead she chooses another. At the end when we see a flashback of that scene, she picks up the first apple she was originally going for.

Monty Python's Flying Circus

Sex and Violence
When commentating on the artists' bicycle race, John Cleese says some more cyclists are approaching and rattles off a very long list of names, but then only three cyclists pass by.

The Naked Ant
In the Upper Class Twit of the Year Show, there are five contestants. However, after Oliver runs himself over, in the events that follow there are only four props for the remaining twits (four mannequins, rabbits, and guns); since Oliver's death was unforeseen, shouldn't there be five of each? This mistake, by the way, is rectified in the film version of this sketch.

Dinsdale

In the 'New Cooker Sketch' Mrs Pinnet says she lives at 46 Algernon Road. When we switch to the exterior shot, the number on the door is 94 and it opens on the other side.

Show 5

In the sketch where Eric Idle plays a milkman/psychiatrist, he visits a woman (Graham Chapman) named Mrs Ratbag. He takes her to the dairy to have a psychiatric examination, and when they get there, her name is now Mrs Pim.

The Spanish Inquisition

During the closing credits while the Spanish Inquisition are going to the Old Bailey, Terry Gilliam is holding a large book. When they burst into the court, he is not.

Murder, She Wrote

Sing a Song of Murder

When Angela Lansbury, playing Emma, was almost hit by a car she jumped up onto the edge of the wall and then down onto the floor. When she landed she was facing the theatre door, but when Oliver came out of the door and the shot changed, she was facing away from the wall. This happened in the transition from stunt person to Angela.

Neighbours

Across whole show

Tahnee and Nina found various copied pictures of Harold with different crazy hairstyles in the trash at Lassiters. When Harold found the original images, there were many pictures of the people from Ramsay Street, but only one of Harold.

Serena and Sky went to the new club called 'Out' but from what you could see of the name outside the club it was obviously not called 'Out'.

Office, The

Episode 2
In Keith's appraisal David asks him about 'The Q & A'. In the shot of Keith answering with 'I thought you filled that in', David's right hand is off the paper. In the next shot his hand is clutching the paper.

Only Fools and Horses

Friday the 14th
When the policeman stops the car, he is seen through the front window of the van, and he has a torch in his left hand. When he moves towards the van he hasn't.

Healthy Competition
Del is escaping in the van and there is a view from the side of the van showing that the door is almost completely shut. But in the next shot, which is a direct view of the back of the van, the door is wide open, allowing space for the toy dogs to fall out of the suitcase and onto the road.

May the Force Be with You
Del is proposing a deal to Slater, who says, 'I don't like deals', and shoves Del's hand off the phone hook (Del was trying to stop

Slater keeping him in custody overnight). But in the next shot Del's hand is still on the hook.

Hole in One
At the beginning of the episode, there is a box by the table Rodney is sitting on. A little later, Albert and Del come and open the box. The box disappears and then reappears between shots.

Tea for Three
Rodney is sitting on the chair and starts eating crisps; you can see that he is sitting on a cushion. It is gone by the time he gets up.

The Longest Night
When Lennox Gilbey opens a can of beer in the supermarket, it can be seen that he has a long purple thing inside his jacket. But he doesn't take that off the shelf until a few shots later.

Red Dwarf

Future Echoes
The sign above the stasis booth in this episode is a different colour from how it was in the previous episode, 'The End'.

Rimmer and Lister go through a door on the left-hand side of the drive room which wasn't there in the previous episode, 'The End'.

Stasis Leak
The first time we see the photograph of Lister and Kochanski married, Lister is smiling in the photo. The second time we see it Lister is not smiling.

Demons & Angels
When Lister swings the axe at The Cat and hits the door frame, the axe head bends. When Lister pulls the axe out, its head is fine again.

The Inquisitor
After the future Kryten cuts off the Inquisitor's hand with the chainsaw, he kicks the glove, which lands about seven feet away from Lister. In the next shot Lister simply bends down and picks the glove up from in front of him.

Gunmen of the Apocalypse
Although four bullets are fired (two from each shooter), only two bullets are heard falling to the floor, and the two bullets we see on the floor are perfectly formed and are not mutilated as they should be from hitting each other in midair.

Back in the Red (1)
The sexual magnetism virus is red in this episode, yet it was a greeny blue colour in 'Quarantine'.

Scrubs

My Journey
When Sean is talking to Betty the seal, his arms go from being by his sides to being clasped in front of him, between shots.

JD throws his clipboard out of the window and the sound of metal hitting metal followed by an alarm can be heard, suggesting it hits a car, so how is it possible that later on JD can be seen treating a patient who claims to have been hit on the head with a clipboard thrown out of a window (JD's)?

Seinfeld

The Cigar Store Indian

George has sex in his parents' bed, explaining, 'My bed is too small.' But, in another episode, we see George's parents' bedroom, and they sleep in twin beds, not a big bed.

The Lip Reader

After Kramer becomes a ballman, Jerry, Elaine and George go to a tennis match at the end of the episode. It shows a shot of the court, and no one is standing anywhere near the poles of the net. In the next shot, Kramer is crouched down next to the pole, ready to dive for the ball.

The Pie

At the end of the episode, Kramer is telling Olive that he met someone else. Olive says, 'Who is she?' and she puts her hand on her hip. In the next shot both hands are back on the kitchen worktop.

George is hoping to buy a discounted suit and there is a scene where he is talking to the foreign shop assistant. In the first shot he has the suit in his hands. The camera switches to the assistant, then back to George, and in the second shot the suit is no longer in his hands.

The Understudy

Bette Midler is injured when George tackles her at home plate. When he hits her, she is knocked into somebody. Yet when they show her again, she is sprawled against the backstop with no one behind or even near her that seems to be hurt.

The Calzone

Towards the end of the episode when George walks in and his boss is looking around for the source of the smell of calzones, George is holding a bag in his hand. In the next shot, which shows the back of the boss's head, the bag is now on top of a box that George is carrying. When it goes back to a close-up the bag is in his hand again.

The Bizarro Jerry

In the scene after 'Man Hands' crushes Jerry's hand, Jerry is wearing a bandage around his hand. But in the next scene on the street, the bandage is gone.

The Soul Mate

George has constructed a model of the boardroom at the time his briefcase was destroyed. Jerry thinks George should be represented by the Yellow M&M figure. When the camera shows a close-up of the figure, Jerry is holding it in a different position than in the faraway shots.

There is a scene where Kramer is talking to Jerry's girlfriend in the library with the help of Newman. Kramer elbows Newman through the shelf, knocking some books down, but in the next shot we see Newman rising and the books are back on the shelf.

Sex and the City

Across whole show

At the beginning of every show we see Carrie walking down the street and getting splashed by the bus. First the bus has people on it, then no one is on it and then, in the last shot as it is driving away, there are people on it.

Secret Sex

Samantha and Carrie are hanging Carrie's poster in her apartment. In one shot, the whole poster is pinned to the wall and in the next shot, the bottom left-hand corner part of the poster is curling up. After another shot of Samantha, the poster is pinned perfectly to the wall again.

Valley of the Twenty-Something Guys

Carrie receives a phone call from Samantha and her voice-over says she needs her morning Marlboro Light; however, when she picks up her pack of cigarettes, you can see that it is a pack of Merits.

Simpsons, The

Across whole show

In the opening to the show, when Marge pulls into the driveway, you can see that there is no badge on the hood of the car, but when it shows a close-up of the front of the car when Homer is running away, there is a grey badge there with a star on it.

Bart the General

When Bart's army is attacking Nelson, there are a lot more kids attacking Nelson than there were training with Bart.

Moaning Lisa

After Homer says, 'I can't concentrate with that infernal racket', the shot moves up onto Lisa's room. From the outside, there is no window frame on the window. But from the inside, there is one going right through the middle.

The Simpsons Christmas Special: Simpsons Roasting on an Open Fire

At the end of an early scene Marge is speaking on the phone to her sisters and they say something that sounds like they said that Homer is ugly. Marge then puts down the phone wire that she was curling round her finger. Weirdly, the phone wire disappears briefly when Marge puts it down.

There's No Disgrace Like Home

The logo in the pawn shop window looks different on the inside than on the outside.

Brush with Greatness

In the scene where Bart and Homer find Marge's paintings in the attic, there is a shot of the paintings all stacked up and you can see that the edges of all of them are the same shade of pink as the front painting. However, when the boys flick through the paintings, the backgrounds and edges are a variety of colours, including pale blue.

When Mr Burns and Smithers go to leave, the beak-like knocker has disappeared from the Simpsons' front door.

Old Money

In the scene where Lionel Hutz hands over the $106 cheque, Abe Simpson's room number is eighteen. After Abe calls Homer, the manager of the Retirement Castle comes in. The number eighteen has now disappeared.

Three Men and a Comic Book

Martin is tied to the chair near the end of the episode and the number of ropes tied to him change from four, to three, and then back to four.

When Martin is tied up in the treehouse, at one point Bart takes the brick off the comic book and sets it down near Martin. When Bart and Milhouse fight, the brick disappears.

Bart the Murderer

After the mobsters enter Skinner's office, the phone on his desk changes position between shots. Also, the name bar on his desk doesn't have anything on it.

Bart puts his lucky red hat on the hat holder. It disappears in the next shot.

There are three mistakes when court is dismissed: 1) the people standing around disappear, 2) the two men with Fat Tony disappear for one shot, and 3) when Bart says that crime doesn't pay, Marge has appeared standing beside Bart.

In the beginning of the episode, when Bart finds that the dog ate his homework, the poster on Bart's door has disappeared for one shot.

Bart realises he forgot his permission slip and the camera shows us that the paper is half-hidden under his pillow. However, when he got out of his bed earlier, the paper wasn't under his pillow.

When Bart sees that Santa's Little Helper ate his homework, and the camera moves really fast, you can see that the Krusty Doll and picture frame have vanished from the desk beside his bed.

Bart leaves home and walks to school. Later, though, he leaves school with his skateboard.

Skinner is set free and, while holding onto the vacuum, he changes position between shots.

We see Skinner's car before the newspapers fall on him; it is a light-brownish colour. When the police arrive, it is the same colour as the cop cars.

After Skinner gets trapped under the papers, the jars on the shelves change colour between shots.

Burns Verkaufen der Kraftwerk

There are several errors in the plant's parking lot: 1) in the overhead shot of the plant, Homer drives in, and there are parking barriers on the road. These disappear in the next shot. 2) As he drives in, there are at least eleven parking spaces on the right side of him. Carl takes up one spot, and in the next shot there are about three parking spaces left. 3) When he parks, several cars are behind him, but in the shot before that, no cars are visible, not even parking spaces, and 4) when both Homer and Carl drive in, there are orange lines on the road, which weren't visible in any other part of the scene.

Homer gets in the car and watches Mr Burns on television, but the lunch box he was just carrying has vanished.

At the Tavern, where Homer slaps the money on the table, the white cloth that Moe was holding has vanished.

In the bar, before Bart stomps on Mr Burns's foot, his back is towards Smithers, but in the next shot, his back is turned towards everyone else.

Before Horst wants to talk with Homer, Lenny, who is standing beside the doughnut box, wasn't seen in the shots before and isn't seen in the shots afterwards.

When Mr Burns shows Smithers the picture of him and Elvis, he is standing beside his desk, which is gone for the rest of the scene.

Colonel Homer
In the scene where Homer decides he wants to stay with Lurlene, she locks the door about three times before going to kiss Homer; but when Homer leaves, he just opens the door without unlocking anything.

Flaming Moe's
At the end of the episode, the barriers outside the Tavern change position.

When Moe tries the Flaming Homer, there are bottles that keep appearing, and the knife disappears suddenly.

Homer enters Moe's Tavern, Moe is playing solitaire. The cards on the table are face down/face up between shots.

Homer Defined
In the shot after Smithers asks Mr Burns where his radiation suit is, Marge's knitting supplies have disappeared.

I Married Marge
When Homer leaves the window, the TV is in a different area of the living room.

When Marge comes into the living room at the end, the Chinese chequers game that Bart and Lisa were just playing is gone.

The Repo Man takes Marge's ring, which is seen on her left hand. It wasn't visible in the shot before.

As Homer and Marge are singing in the car, there is one exterior shot showing that the car is yellow, but in the rest of the scene it is green.

Before Homer and Marge get married, they walk much further than the actual length of the aisle, as can be seen from the interior of the wedding chapel shown before this scene.

Like Father, Like Klown

When Bart writes the letter to Krusty, most of the objects on the table have disappeared.

At the beginning of this episode, when Krusty does his axe-throwing act on Sideshow Mel, the number of axes on the board changes from four to five.

Krusty dials '1-909-SEX-CHAT', but he presses '90190' on the phone.

Krusty tells the monkey to wait in the car. However, when Krusty leaves, he has no car.

When Bart and Lisa see Reverend Lovejoy, their chairs keep moving closer then separating, between shots.

During Krusty's performance, the tables change from round to long and rectangular.

Lisa's Pony

When Homer is phoned by Lisa, the colour of the phone is blue. Immediately after, it turns to green.

In the last shot of Marge and Homer's discussion about buying a pony, we can see a door on the right side of the screen. This door changes position when Lisa rides in the bedroom with her pony.

During Lisa's performance in the talent show, in one shot of the audience we see, from left to right: Ned Flanders, Maude Flanders and another lady. For the rest of the show we see that Jasper is sitting where the lady was.

Mr Lisa Goes to Washington

As Lisa approaches the Abe Lincoln statue, there is an old person near her. In the next shot, there are three people surrounding her.

Radio Bart

While Rod and Todd talk to 'God' on the radio, the antenna keeps changing position for the entire scene.

In the scene where Bart tries to get his radio back from the well, watch the police barriers. When Lou and Eddie get coffee, they walk through one of the barriers, tearing it. Several shots later, this torn piece has vanished, and then the barriers disappear entirely.

Saturdays of Thunder

Homer jumps into the car having completed the Fatherhood test and drives off to see Bart race. The car shifts from reverse to forward without Homer moving a gear stick.

Before the time trials start, the audience on the sidelines keep disappearing and reappearing.

While Homer helps Bart with his racer, the wall of the inside of the garage keeps changing from blue to red.

In the garage, Martin walks behind Lewis and the other kid. He is walking in front of them in the next shot.

Patty sprays Barney with pepper spray. It disappears from her hand in the next shot.

As Nelson crosses the finishing line at the time trials, the front piece of wood on Bart's car breaks off. It is attached to the car again in the next shot.

When Nelson is handed the knife by his two friends, Martin, Bart and their cars have disappeared for two shots. Then they reappear as before.

Separate Vocations

In the scene where Miss Hoover asks Lisa what the nineteenth-century figure nicknamed 'Old Hickory' is, there is no text on the covers of the book she's holding. In the next two shots, however, 'Teacher's Edition' can be seen on the front cover and the spine of the book.

As Bart and Skinner are checking lockers, you can see in a wide shot that Bart needs to check six lockers before he gets to Lisa's locker. However, Bart checks eight lockers and then opens Lisa's locker.

When the mean girls try to get Lisa out of the bad girls' washroom, the magazine that one of the girls was carrying disappears. The cigarette that the other girl was holding also vanishes.

Stark Raving Dad
After Marge finds out that Bart didn't watch Maggie, Maggie spits her pacifier at him. In the very next shot her pacifier is back in her mouth.

Mr Burns notices that Homer is wearing a pink shirt to work. He pauses and zooms in the video, with Homer looking almost directly at the camera. In the next shot, though, he is looking more to his left. There are different people surrounding him too.

The Otto Show
At the end of the episode, when the kids are lined up to wait to see whether Otto is back driving the bus, there are several shots that switch back and forth between a direct view of the kids and a shot from behind. Lisa changes position between shots.

Tree House of Horror II: A Simpsons Halloween
At the beginning of part one, between the first two shots, Lisa is in a different position, and Marge has vanished.

At the beginning of the episode, when Jimbo and Kearney take Homer's candy, the door knocker is gone in the first shot. There is also a peephole on the inside of the door, but this is never visible from the outside.

When Homer purchases the monkey's paw, you can see open desert to the right of Homer. There was a building in its place a few shots earlier.

When the aliens land in Springfield, the number and positions of the people in front of the Jebediah statue change between shots.

As the family looks out the window to see the limo, the light switch on the wall has vanished.

Itchy and Scratchy: The Movie

Bart runs to the ticket booth, which has no one inside it. However, somebody appears there when he tries to buy a ticket.

Marge Gets a Job

The family is at dinner and there is a top-down view which zooms in on them from above. In this shot there is no newspaper on the chest (to Homer's left). In the next shot of Homer a newspaper has appeared.

When Mr Burns draws the moustache and horns on the image of Marge on the TV screen, they just disappear in the next shot when he starts to draw the bees.

Homer's Barbershop Quartet

When you see a shot of the church from outside in the scene where the Bee Sharps sing there, look closely at the sign. You will see that it says 'Also: The Bee Sharps', but they don't name themselves that until later on in the episode.

At the sale, when Bart and Lisa first find 'The Bee Sharps' album, the order of the records in the stack changes in subsequent shots.

Secrets of a Successful Marriage

Marge is shopping at the Kwik-E-Mart and she puts a red can and a blue can on the counter. When Apu tells her about the offer on hair dye he puts two blue cans into the paper bag.

Sweet Seymour Skinner's Baadasssss Song
Near the beginning of the episode, Bart is thinking what it would be like to get out of school. You can see his desk quite well and there is nothing on it. But when Bart has finished thinking, a piece of paper has appeared on his desk.

Bart of Darkness
Bart is watching Rod and Todd walk over to Ned Flanders and their reflections can be seen on Bart's telescope. Their reflections do not match their actual positions.

Bart vs. Australia
When Bart and Lisa are looking at the globe, Bart points out Argentina and 'Ran McNally'. Next time you see the globe, it is showing Africa and Asia, but Asia is shown incorrectly and the equator has disappeared.

Homer is threatening to boot the Prime Minister and is holding him still with his left arm. When the shot comes from behind Homer, he has his right arm on the Prime Minister's shoulder. When the shot cuts back to a direct view of Homer, his right arm isn't touching the PM.

Bart's Comet
At the end of the episode, when we see a wide shot of everyone going to join Ned on the hill (and singing the song), look to the far left. You will see Apu – his skin is yellow.

Homer vs. Patty and Selma
When Bart takes off his face mask during his ballet performance, all of his fellow dancers have disappeared.

Homie the Clown
In the last scene when Homer is about to attempt the loop trick, it is seen several times that the Mafia guys are not standing in a straight line. Then when Homer fails, then says 'Ta da', they are shown head to head in a straight line.

Springfield Connection
In the police station the blue light on the ceiling disappears after the police are seen laughing at Marge.

When Marge is shopping, there is a blue baby seat in her trolley. In a following shot of her running with the trolley and it going into the cheese display, the seat has gone.

Marge is making celery soup and the front view of her shows only the chopping board in front of her. Then, when Lisa talks to her, the microwave is seen in front of her.

The police pull up outside the station and park three cars in front of the entrance and in front of the steps. In the next shot the cars are apart on the road, and then, when Marge walks by them, they are in a line to the side of the steps.

Who Shot Mr Burns? (1)
While Burns is pretending to be a student in Skinner's office, the door changes from open to closed and from dark blue/green to grey.

Who Shot Mr Burns? (2)
When Smithers realises that he shot Jasper, instead of Mr Burns, he mentions that he left the meeting early in order to watch *Pardon My Zinger*. However, in the previous episode, you see him walk out of the meeting with everyone else, very slowly.

Bart After Dark
Marge goes to see Belle at the Maison Derriere and sits down with her. At first there is a white ornament on the small table in front of them but then, at the end of the scene, it has vanished.

You Only Move Twice
While the family are talking and Marge is sitting on the sofa, Bart runs and shoves Lisa (who is in front of Marge) out of the way but, in the next shot, she is still in front of Marge, despite the fact Bart pushed her out of his way.

Realty Bites
When Marge finds out that Mr Hutz does real estate, the FOR SALE sign changes from black to red and then back again.

This Little Wiggy
At the end of the episode, when Mr Burns rotates his desk to turn off the power, the ink block and fountain pen to his left change position.

In the scene at the abandoned penitentiary the puddle which Ralph and Bart fall into appears from nowhere.

When Chief Wiggum finally climbs the stairs his gun is seen to be a black, old-style revolver with a curved handle. In the next shot, where he draws his gun, it is a grey, new-style handgun.

Mr Burns opens the note from the rocket and places the rubber band on his desk. In a following shot the rubber band changes position.

Ralph and Bart are playing cards; Ralph has four cards in his hand. In following shots he first has five cards then back to four again.

The family are on the conveyer belt in the Knowledgeium when Homer turns round and grabs the handrail (after the Troy McClure announcement) and his fingers are just touching the rail. In the next shot his hands are clasped to the rail.

At the penitentiary gates, Nelson's position changes between shots. The whole group are near the gates, then far away, then Nelson is separate from the group when he throws the key.

In the Wiggums' house the parents' bedroom changes style several times. It is first seen when Chief Wiggum is looking into the room after climbing the stairs and the cupboard is opposite the door. Then, later, when Chief Wiggum enters the room it is on the wall running across from the doorway. When the Chief puts the police master key on his bed post the doorway is behind the bed and the bed is opposite the cupboard. Later, when Bart steals the key, the bed is seen parallel to the doorway.

As soon as the family has left the Knowledgeium, they are immediately outside walking away. The shot changes and the building is nowhere to be seen.

In the scene where the bullies are talking to Bart and Ralph on the street corner, they move positions between shots. They change from being in a straight line to being in an arc shape, to being in a group.

The Old Man and the C Student

Springy the Olympic spring that Homer makes has nine coils. Then we see the large version that has many coils at the Olympics meeting. Homer's original spring is in his hand and now it has many coils also. A cut back to the stage shows the large spring has few coils, like the first time we saw Springy.

Days of Wine and D'Oh'ses
In the video of Barney's birthday, there is a shot of Barney being handcuffed to a police car. This causes Barney to realise where it came from and to lift his arm, with the door from the police car attached to it. However, in shots up until that point, Barney's arm has had nothing attached to it.

Guess Who's Coming to Criticise Dinner
All the people who are plotting to murder Homer are talking about the reviews Homer has given them. The Japanese man says, 'so why did you put yours in the window?' and you see the review. At the end of that scene, when they are all laughing, you see the building they are in, and it has nothing in the window.

Tree House of Horror X
The broken railing in front of Lucy Lawless returns to normal when the shot changes after the Collector lands on the computer.

Children of a Lesser Clod
When Ned Flanders is asking Homer whether or not he is running a day care centre, you can see that there is a radio behind him. The aerial on it changes position in subsequent shots.

Lisa the Tree Hugger
Bart's magazine appears in the second shot of him and Lisa talking; it's not in the first.

Skinner's Sense of Snow
When the hamster, Nibbles, has rolled back to Skinner, it takes the lid of the ball off, and the lid lands on the ground. When the hamster is rolling away from Skinner it doesn't put the lid back

on, it just leaves it on the ground, but in the next shot the lid has suddenly disappeared.

Tennis the Menace
At the beginning of the episode, Bart places Santa's Little Helper's dish into the sink and begins playing with the taps. Marge comes in, the bowl magically disappears from the sink and it's missing for the rest of the scene.

Homer the Moe
When Homer opens up his bar there are four cars parked outside. Later, when Moe opens the garage door there are no cars, but no one has left.

Jaws Wired Shut
In the cinema, it is clear that the people attending the movie keep on changing. For example, for a few shots, you can see that Krabappel and Skinner are sitting in the front row, but the next time you see those seats, they have been replaced by Lenny and Carl, and Krabappel and Skinner aren't in sight.

The Blunder Years
At the end of the episode, Homer puts a skull in a box on the coffee table. When Moe arrives to explain his theory, first the box disappears from the coffee table, then the entire table vanishes.

'Tis the Fifteenth Season
When we first see the skating rink, it has Jasper, Disco Stu, Otto, Apu and Manjua, Sideshow Mel, a couple of children and two couples skating on it. In the next shot we see the Comic Store Guy split his trousers – he wasn't there before.

Diatribe of a Mad Housewife
In the first shot of the book-reading, Ms Krabappel is sitting at the end of the row. The next time, Groundskeeper Willie is there. The third time we see the audience, Apu has appeared in the front row as well.

I, (Annoyed Grunt)-bot
As the boys reach the top of the hill the light on the front of the bike has shrunk dramatically since the first time we saw it in Bart's driveway.

The remote control for the robot in Bart's bedroom appears from nowhere.

The cats' graves change position. When Snowball II is buried, they're away from the tree and near the fence. When Snowball III is buried, the graves are away from the fence and Snowball is among the roots of the tree.

The jagged piece of metal that Homer pulls from his arm disappears from the bedside table in the very next shot.

Marge vs. Singles, Seniors, Childless Couples and Teens, and Gays
Homer sneaks into Maggie's room (to smash the CD player), where there is a yellow box with musical notes painted on it. The notes are different in each shot.

When Bart asks Ms Krabappel for detention, the piece of paper on his desk disappears.

Today, I am a Klown
After Homer pushes in front of Lisa in the queue for the

bathroom, she loses the toothbrush she was holding in her left hand.

When Homer leaves the studio after his show is cancelled there is no sign next to the door. When Marge walks up to comfort him there is now a 'stage door' sign there.

While Krusty is describing his prostate to the children, the green umbrella vanishes from beside Lisa.

Sopranos, The

Amour Fou
Towards the end of the episode Carmela is reading a book on real estate. When a close-up of the book is shown, she is at the beginning of chapter one, yet when the camera angle changes she is about halfway through the book.

Pie-O-My
While standing outside the horse's stall, Ralphie's arms go from being at his sides, to folded across his chest throughout the whole scene.

A different horse is used for close-ups and race shots; you can tell by the white patch on Pie-O-My's head, which is much bigger in the close-ups.

South Park

An Elephant Makes Love to a Pig
In the final classroom scene, whenever they show Kyle, he is in front of the class, but in the wide shots, he is behind other kids.

Big Gay Al's Big Gay Boat Ride
During the football game, the announcer says, 'And the ball is passed to twenty-three, Kenny McCormick.' But Kenny's number is thirteen.

Rainforest Schmainforest
A little while after Cartman leaves the group and finds the construction zone, a frontal view of the rest of the group is shown. Cartman is still in it.

Butters' Very Own Episode
As we view Butters from the front of the car, the clip of his seatbelt is above the seat, but when the shot changes to a close-up of Butters, the clip is below the top of the seat.

Proper Condom Use
During the first classroom scene, Token is in the back with Kenny partially in front of him, but in the close-up of the projector with Token in front of it, we don't see Kenny anywhere.

Free Hat
When George is seen from outside his house, there is nothing but clear glass, but when he is seen from inside, there is a black rail across the glass at about waist level.

It's Christmas in Canada
During the Christmas tree lighting, when Mr Garrison is suggesting that the town get rid of all Mexicans, the people standing in front of him change from shot to shot.

Star Trek: The Next Generation

The Emissary

In the beginning of the episode, Riker, Geordi, Worf, Data and Pulaski are playing poker. Pulaski puts two neat stacks of chips in the centre beside some chips in a pile. Worf is then shown putting similar stacks in the centre but Pulaski's stacks are not visible and they should be. Then, when Worf wins the hand, the camera is showing a wide shot of him pulling the chips towards him and you can see his and Pulaski's neat stacks of chips.

That '70s Show

Punk Chick

This episode was supposed to air before 'The Water Tower', but was actually shown after it. In this episode, when Eric tries to talk some sense into Hyde about moving to New York he says, 'we were going to paint a pot-leaf on the water tower', which they already did in the episode before.

Donna's Story

Jackie enters the basement and says 'great story' while she is holding the newspaper by the sides. In the next shot, while the gang is laughing, she is now holding it by the bottom.

Will & Grace

Guess Who's Not Coming to Dinner

Karen arrives for Grace's dinner party and walks across the blanket Grace has set up and scatters some dishes. They talk for a moment, and when you next see the blanket, the dishes are back in place, yet neither Grace nor Karen has touched them.

. . . And the Horse He Rode in On

While in the coffee shop, Leo writes Grace a 'prescription'. As she is reading the piece of paper, Leo puts the prescription pad back into his shirt pocket. In the next shot the pad is on the table in front of him.

Dames at Sea

When Grace reads Dr Morty's letter on Karen's boat (during the last episode of Season Five) it sounds at least a few paragraphs in length. During this episode, when she holds the letter up (when speaking to Will and later to Leo) there is only a short paragraph on the bordered side of the page, and nothing on the other side.

ONCE MORE UNTO THE BREACH

Another side effect of editing – have you ever noticed that if a word is printed at the end of one line, and then is repeated at the start of the next, that you skip straight over it without it really registering? The same happens in TV shows – if a character repeats the same movement in two different shots it'll often slip right past you, unless you pay attention . . .

Boy Meets World

Singled Out
The same girls keep leaving the stage every time Eric answers a question.

Buffy the Vampire Slayer

Angel
In the best tradition of old Western movies, Darla seems to have a limitless supply of bullets in the final shoot-out – despite never reloading her guns.

Nightmares
Buffy is talking to Willow about her mom's divorce and she shuts her locker. A few seconds later she shuts her locker again.

The Dark Age
When Buffy and Giles are talking in the school in the final scene, the same extra (in a beige shirt and blue jeans) walks out of the room behind Buffy twice.

When She Was Bad

In the scene where Buffy smashes the master's skeleton with a sledgehammer, she smashes the ribcage to pieces. Suddenly the ribcage has again become completely intact and she smashes it to hell again.

The Wish

Buffy is walking forwards through Angel's dust and there's a vampire running towards her; he is only a few steps behind her. Then there's a shot of her walking forwards taken from another angle; when we can see behind her again, the same vampire hasn't moved forwards at all, he's still running from three steps behind her.

Friends

The One with the Prom Video

The group have just finished watching the prom video and the TV screen goes blank because it is finished. Monica has been sitting next to Rachel. In the reflection of the TV screen you can see her beginning to stand up. We cut back to a 'real' view, and she's sitting down, then she stands up again.

The One with the Dollhouse

When Chandler is in Rachel's office, she tells him the lingerie isn't kept there. He says, 'yes I realise that', and starts reaching for the catalogue she's about to give him. The camera cuts, and he's now standing with his hands in his pockets, reaching out again when she gives him the catalogue.

The One with the Tiny T-Shirt

Ross is over at Chandler and Joey's looking through the peephole for hours waiting for Rachel to return. When she does and

Ross sees her go inside with Mark, Ross tries to open the door to go to see her, and Chandler jumps on his back to stop him. As Chandler says, 'I. . . am not going to let you do this', Ross grabs the door handle. Then the angle changes, and as Chandler says, 'You . . . are surprisingly strong,' Ross is further from the handle and grabs it again.

The One with All the Kissing
There is a scene in Central Perk where Rachel confronts Chandler about all the kissing he's been doing. She raises her hands up in front of her and tells Chandler to hold on to stop him from getting up from the couch. As he goes to sit back down on the couch she lowers her hands to her lap. The shot cuts to an angle behind Rachel's chair and she is lowering her hands again.

The One with Joey's Bag
When Phoebe is in the coffee house talking to her father and pretending to be the executor of her grandmother's will, after she says 'lipstick and a daughter, big day for you', she folds her papers in half, but in the next shot they are unfolded and she then folds them again.

The One where Rachel Has a Baby, Part 1
The couple who have unpleasant pet names for each other are sharing the maternity room with Rachel; the man is unpacking a suitcase that he closes, but in the next shot it's open and he flips the top closed again.

The One with the Video Tape
When the six of them are watching Ross and Rachel on the TV and when Rachel (on the video) is discussing the invitations and

how Monica didn't shut up about sending them, Chandler points at the TV and makes a kind-of confused face. A short while later, just before he says 'Did you do it on our invitations?' the same shot of him pointing and pulling a face comes up.

The One with Phoebe's Rats

Phoebe is in her apartment explaining about giving up the triplets she had for her brother and she puts the box down on the table, yet when it cuts to Mike's face and Phoebe's realisation that she hadn't told him that before, the box is back on her lap.

The One with the Mugging

Phoebe brings her 'crap from the street' box to the coffee shop to show Ross, and she opens the flaps of the box twice.

Malcolm in the Middle

Pilot

When Lois hangs up on Francis before saying 'Oh, I love you', it seems as though the line is already disconnected (as can be heard from the dial tone from Francis' side), but in a later shot, Malcolm and Reese are just about to hang up the phone.

Only Fools and Horses

Healthy Competition

Del is trying to sell those hooky toy dogs and there are some shots of the policeman walking across the street. The same clip of that policeman is played twice, only one is longer than the other (note a grey-haired man walk across the screen twice).

Simpsons, The

Saturdays of Thunder

At the institute, Dave puts his hand on his son twice, and they also swap positions between shots.

Separate Vocations

Watch carefully and you will see the same footage of Bart and Skinner slamming locker doors is used. The easiest shots to spot it in are those of Bart from inside a locker, where a kid's scrapbook is on the left-hand side.

THE SHOW MUST GO ON

Of course all the action in any show normally takes place in the foreground. But just how often do you pay close attention to all the little bits of scenery and movement which programme makers think you'll ignore? Start ignoring the stars and peering behind them, and you may be surprised what you can see . . .

Alias

The Prophecy

When Roger Moore is showing Sloane the bank accounts, he says, 'five deposits in excess of forty-five million dollars. . .', but the shot just before that shows deposits of (in thousands), \$9,362, \$7,215, \$9,010, \$8,300, and \$9,250. That makes \$43,137,000, which isn't in excess of \$45 million.

Angel

Darla

While Angel is talking to Darla on the phone there is a shot of Cordy, Wes and Gunn and you can see Cordy unfold her arms; but when it goes back to Angel you can see Cordelia in the background, and her arms are crossed again.

Band of Brothers

Currahee

The door keeps changing positions in the scene where Sobel is punishing Winters for failing to inspect the latrine.

Black Adder

Beer

The door to the dining room is open when Edmund is throwing his drink in the cupboard. Then, when he returns after directing Queenie into the cupboard, it is closed. He closed it when he left the room to answer the door, so it should have been closed the whole time.

Just after Edmund has 'locked' the door on Queenie, it comes open when he walks away from it. There is even the sound of the door opening.

Boy Meets World

By Hook or By Crook

When Eric is talking to his tutor in the hallway after receiving an A– on a test, there is a poster in the background for Sex Ed. This changes though, from saying 'Sex, Ed?' to 'Sex Ed' throughout the scene.

Pairing Off

At the end of this episode, when Eric and Cory are talking about Cory's date, Eric walks from his desk to the bed and we see the bedroom door is open, but when he walks back to his desk, the door is closed.

Truth and Consequences

When they catch Janitor Bud on tape, there is a time clock on the wall. Through the rest of the episode there isn't.

Buffy the Vampire Slayer

Teacher's Pet

Doctor Gregory is giving the class a lecture about ants. But he projects an image of a beetle onto the wall behind him. Shouldn't he know the difference?

Becoming (1)

As Buffy kneels over Kendra's corpse the door can be seen over her shoulder; it stays closed all the time. There is then a cut to a shot of Buffy from behind, showing a cop raising his gun, but he couldn't have come through the door without being visible in the last shot.

I Only Have Eyes for You

After Buffy has entered the wasp-filled school there's a shot of Giles, Willow and Xander standing outside waiting for her. In the establishing long shot look closely and you can see they used stock footage of the group – the blatant giveaway is that Buffy is standing there with them . . . waiting for Buffy to come out.

Killed By Death

When Buffy looks into the childrens' ward the sign on the door saying BASEMENT ACCESS is seen in some shots but disappears completely in others.

Graduation Day (1)

Buffy and Faith are fighting; Faith falls into a table which has comics on it. She knocks every single one of them onto the floor. In one or two later shots it can be seen (at the very edge of the screen) that there's still a comic on the table.

Doomed

During the fight at the Hellmouth, Willow throws the sack of bones to Spike, who catches them and looks startled. In the very next shot of Buffy fighting one of the demons, Spike can be seen in the upper left corner of the screen, with empty hands, quite calmly watching the fight.

Shadow

When Glory creates the demon snake thing, we see a computer-generated image of the creature, but Glory and Buffy are nowhere to be seen. When we are shown where they are standing, it is clear their position should have been visible when the snake demon was created.

Once More, with Feeling

Buffy is singing her final song in the Bronze; Tara and Anya are standing in the background watching. Look closely and you will see their hands keep changing from crossed to uncrossed between shots.

Get It Done

When Dawn and Buffy find Chloe's corpse, the door across the hall from them is open. When it cuts back to them after the ad break it is shut, but there has been no time lapse.

Dawson's Creek

All Good Things . . . (1)

Near the beginning of the episode, when Jack is pulled over, the creek behind him is empty and remains like that throughout the scene. Then, for the last few shots before he drives off again, a sailboat has appeared in the background, seemingly out of nowhere.

Family Guy

And the Wiener is . . .

While Peter and Lois talk about Meg, there is no one behind them. In the next shot of them, after the meat has been shot at Meg, there is a whole crowd of people sitting in the bleachers directly behind them.

Friends

The One where Underdog Gets Away

Whenever Monica's apartment is shot from the point of view of the balcony, looking in, fake walls have to be put up across the room to cover the open space (since there is no wall there usually, just the audience). When the friends are looking out of the window at Ugly Naked Guy and his girlfriend in this episode, it is evident that the rear wall does not extend nearly far enough – there is a large black space behind Monica.

The One After the Superbowl, Part 2

Chandler is talking to Susie (Julia Roberts) and there is a man standing behind Chandler in a doorway. It cuts to Susie, but when the camera goes back to Chandler the man is not there. Then he appears again.

The One where Old Yeller Dies

Chandler and Joey are spending time with Richard. As they play foosball and Richard scores, he leans back and says, in a mockery of Chandler, 'Could that shot BE any prettier?' and you can see the end of the wall and the hallway behind it (the wall set ends).

The One where Monica and Richard Are Just Friends

Monica and Richard are squishing tomatoes. When she starts dabbing his shirt with club soda, the door behind them leading to Monica's room goes from open to shut between two shots.

The One with the Race Car Bed

When Joey is teaching soap opera for actors, the 'a' in his name on the board changes from being on the line to being above it. The line itself also reaches the far right of the board in some shots, and is short of it in others.

The One with Rachel's Crush

In this episode, Monica cleans her and Rachel's 'new' apartment (which used to belong to the guys). She even goes as far as to pull the carpet up and polish the wooden floor underneath. When she invites everyone to see the new, clean apartment, she asks if anyone notices anything different about the floor. When Joey says no, she says, 'You used to have carpet.' But at the start of this episode, when Rachel comes in, you can see a bit of the floor by the door, and the wood is already showing. Some carpet is visible in a more obvious area.

The One in Vegas, Part 2

When Monica and Chandler find the dice under the craps table, it is at an angle so both the four and five appear up. But when the camera changes to the last shot (the zoom-in of them kissing) you can see the dice sitting flat on the floor.

The One with the Ball

In the interrogation room, the blinds behind Phoebe keep going from open to closed in different shots.

The One with All the Cheesecakes

Chandler walks into the apartment to find Rachel eating cheese-cake without him. As the door is shutting, the pen on the Magna doodle thing is hanging loose. You can hear it hit the door when he is closing it. In the next shot Rachel stops eating but when we cut back to Chandler the door is closed and the pen is in its holder.

The One with the Rumour

The gang confront Ross over his affair with a fifty-year-old librarian when he was younger. If you watch the mirror behind him (in one of the girls' rooms), it changes angles every time the camera cuts between Ross and the rest of the gang.

The One in Barbados, Part 2

When Monica and Mike play table tennis and Monica says, 'I think that may have missed the table', there is no one sitting in the chairs behind her. The shot then cuts to Mike and he replies 'oh do you?' A further cut to Monica as she replies 'er, yeah' shows there are two people sitting in the chairs behind her.

The One where No One Proposes

In the scene where Rachel believes Joey has proposed to her at the hospital after having Emma, Ross is talking to Rachel about her saying yes to Joey's proposal. The nurse brings Emma in to breast feed. When the nurse leaves, she closes the door. However, when they cut back to Joey a couple of times before he leaves the room, the door is open.

The One with Rachel's Other Sister

While Amy and Rachel are arguing in Monica and Chandler's apartment, the door behind Amy leading to the guest room changes from open to closed in almost every shot.

M*A*S*H

M*A*S*H – The Pilot

When Hawkeye and Trapper are arrested by Hammond at the party, there is a large crowd of people behind the General and Henry. When we cut to the shot of Margaret and Frank approaching, there is no one in sight.

Hanky Panky

When Hawkeye is trying to find out whether there is anything going on between BJ and Nurse Donovan, one of two jackets behind him disappears and the other moves to the other side of him.

Only Fools and Horses

Healthy Competition

Just before Del says that Rodney needs Radar, the door behind Rodney is beginning to swing open. Nobody makes any move to close it. The next time we see that door, it is firmly shut.

Red Dwarf

Parallel Universe

In the quarters of the female versions of the crew, the newspaper clippings and certificates on the wall still have the name 'Arnold' on them, and not the female equivalent, as it was supposed to be.

Simpsons, The

Across whole show

This is in the introduction for the later episodes. When Homer screams, he turns round. You see this in a wide shot. There are no boxes to the right of the door in the garage. However, two appear out of thin air when he runs through the garage.

Homer vs. Lisa and the 8th Commandment
Homer is imagining being locked in the jail cell but he turns around to find he is in his own home. He turns to look at his family. There is a close-up shot of his terrified face, and the people in the background watching the game (it might be Lenny and Karl) have no eyes. Their faces are fine, but their eyes are missing.

Bart the Murderer
When the newspapers fall on Skinner, the rake in the corner has turned into a shovel.

When the pile of newspapers fall on Principal Skinner, two garbage cans appear out of nowhere beside the door.

Burns Verkaufen der Kraftwerk
When Carl complains that he can't be fired, everybody behind him, Homer and Lenny has disappeared.

Flaming Moe's
At the end of the episode, when Homer apologises to Moe, he comes in while the door is left open. It remains closed for the rest of the scene.

Homer Defined
When the salt spills on Milhouse's food, the table full of kids in the background has disappeared.

Look carefully in Mr Burns's surveillance cameras – the workers are identical.

At the beginning of the episode, when the bus is driving to the school, the street lights outside disappear and reappear between shots.

I Married Marge
In the flashback, when Marge's sisters start smoking, there is only one ledge on the wall behind them. In the next shot there are three ledges and a clock.

Like Father, Like Klown
When Krusty does his performance in front of the Rabbis, Krusty's father starts talking to another Rabbi, and a third Rabbi is seen at another table in the background. In the next two shots this Rabbi has vanished.

Lisa's Pony
The people sitting behind Marge during the talent show keep changing/disappearing.

When Homer tells the family where the horse will be kept, look in the background and you will see there are drapes on the wall. These drapes weren't visible when Marge and Homer walked into the kitchen.

Saturdays of Thunder
In the video store, where Homer looks at sports tapes, the categories of movies behind him change in order from drama, horror and 'Elvis', to drama, Western and horror.

The Otto Show

As Otto is playing the guitar with Bart in the middle of the night, there are close-ups of Otto whenever he is singing. The wall behind him is plain. However, when there is a wide shot of Otto and Bart, the wall behind Otto has two tables leaning against it.

When Skinner is calmly driving the bus on the way to school, he has obviously gone past a number of power lines, which can be seen in the background. However, when Skinner is trying to get onto the main road, the power lines have disappeared from the background.

Tree House of Horror II: A Simpsons Halloween

Lisa declares world peace and the two UN guys hug each other, but the United Nations symbol on the wall, which previously had no ocean showing, now has the continents and the ocean in a circle.

Itchy and Scratchy: The Movie

Before the Simpsons are in their house talking about the Itchy and Scratchy movie, there's a line of people waiting to see it that extends past their house and down numerous streets. When it shows one of the kids talking, the window behind them shows that all the people have vanished.

Lisa the Beauty Queen

When it is announced that Amber is the winner of the contest, and Lisa is runner-up, the stands in the back of the stage are empty. However, when Lisa walks off, all the contestants are back on the stands.

Lisa's First Word

Even though Grandpa Simpson is younger in this episode, a picture of his older self is hanging in the Simpsons' home. Creepy.

Homer Goes to College
The colour of the alien poster in the nerds' room changes from pink to blue.

Who Shot Mr Burns? (1)
Early on in this episode, Mr Burns says something like 'this positively has to be there overnight', the shot getting closer on every word or so. The background behind Mr Burns is the Plant but, when the shot zooms out, the background is now one of the corridors.

Bart Carny
The Simpsons arrive back at their house and discover that the two carnival workers they let live with them have boarded up every window and way into the house. However, when they are in the tree house, it can be seen that the windows on the upper floor have remained unboarded.

New Kids on the Blecch
While Homer is pinching Lisa with the 'jealousy bug', the sign behind him changes from a gift store to an antique store.

I, (Annoyed Grunt)-bot
When Snowball III drowns, the number of weeds and rocks in the fish tank changes between shots.

Today, I am a Klown
Krusty enters the Jewish Walk of Fame building; there are no stars on the pavement outside it. When he leaves there are.

When Krusty ends up in his old neighbourhood, the street changes between shots. For instance the 'LLBeanie' sign appears above the door of the second shop and the suit of the man reading the newspaper changes from grey to blue.

South Park

Pink Eye

At the end of the episode when the aeroplane hits Kenny, there is a gravestone with a cross on it behind him, but when the other three boys were talking, none of the gravestones behind them had crosses.

LIGHTS, CAMERA, ACTION!

Much like crew members ending up in shot, cameras, lights and microphones can be unwieldy beasts which have an unfortunate tendency to creep into shot when people least expect it . . .

Alias

Q and A

In the first run through of Sydney driving into the dock in the car, look closely in the long shot and you will see that the cable being used to pull the car is visible. Presumably safer than a stunt driver . . .

Are You Being Served?

A Change Is as Good as a Rest

In the opening scene in the boardroom when Mr Lucas is commenting on how Mrs Slocombe is 'big in the south', you can see the shadow of a boom mike floating back and forth across the table.

Buffy the Vampire Slayer

Phases

Immediately after Kane and Buffy's fight in the woods, in the shot right after Kane leaves, set-lights are visible above the clearing where they fought.

Graduation Day (1)

When Faith shoots Angel with the longbow, you can see the false point spring out from inside his jacket, as if it were on a hinge. Which, let's be honest, it is.

Revelations

In the Buffy and Faith fight about the time Buffy says, 'We can work this out . . .', you can see what appears to be a boom mike bob in and out of the frame in the top left corner.

Hush

The demons known as 'The Gentlemen' always float about two inches off the ground. In one scene, two of them are moving through a park, but the light-blue cart they are standing on can be seen. It was probably meant to be removed via blue-screen technique in post-production but overlooked.

Into the Woods

At the very end of this episode you see shots of Buffy and Riley from both the helicopter and the ground. In the second shot of the helicopter a camera near the top right corner of the chopper is visible.

Villains

As Willow is chasing Warren through the forest, trees move out of her way to let her pass. When the trees behind her move back into place, in one shot you can see the rope used to tug one of the trees down.

Farscape

Unrealised Reality (1)

When Crichton is about to take his last journey into the wormhole (in this episode at least) he pulls down the visor of his helmet.

We can see four white lights, both square and round, reflected, that are not from the current scene.

Fawlty Towers

The Germans
Basil is running from the restaurant and into the office. As the door opens to the hallway a monitor can be seen in the office, showing the action. The director must be watching from in there.

The Psychiatrist
When Basil is trying to explain to Sybil about the woman in the guest's room, the shadow of a boom mike appears on the top wall.

Friends

The One with a Chick. And a Duck.
Monica is talking to Pete in the diner when he gets back from Japan. On the floor at Monica's end of the counter at the very beginning of the scene, lies the mat that is there to protect her when she falls over later.

The One with the Hypnosis Tape
When Monica leaves the apartment with Pete and everyone is watching, the stage lights on the ceiling show up in shots from Pete's viewpoint.

The One with the Baby Shower
At the end of the episode, Monica chases after Rachel's mom to apologise and she falls over. The safety mat, which is blue and just down the first step, is clearly seen to move when Monica falls on to it.

The One with the Cooking Class
Just after Ross gets back from his date, a boom mike is hovering over Rachel's head.

The One with Ross's Inappropriate Song
Chandler is watching the tape he found at Richard's. He is worried that Monica is on it. Joey tackles him to the ground to stop him seeing it. When Monica comes home Joey pulls her down on top of Chandler to stop *her* seeing it. You can see a protective pad on Monica's knee, under her skirt.

Monty Python's Flying Circus

Oh, You're No Fun Anymore
At the beginning of the 'Camel Spotting' sketch the shadow of the boom mike moves back and forth over Eric Idle.

Sex and Violence
In the opening scene, when Graham Chapman sits on a pig, the shadow of the microphone is visible on the wall behind him.

Only Fools and Horses

If They Could See Us Now . . .!
When Del is on the TV show *Goldrush*, he asks to phone Rodney to help him out on a question. As Rodney is watching the show and listening, you can see the camera reflected in Rodney's TV.

Red Dwarf

Kryten
When the crew are in their sleeping quarters, and Rimmer is

talking to the others, a boom mike can be seen hovering over his head.

Bodyswap
In the scene where Rimmer (in Lister's body) pretends to have lost an arm, there is a visible shadow of the boom mike on the wall to his left.

Marooned
Look closely when the camera follows Lister (in the scene just before the meteor crashes onto Starbug) and you will see the edge of the set and some studio lights.

Gunmen of the Apocalypse
After the simulant has beamed on board Starbug, Lister and The Cat get up slowly from the table. Look closely, and you can see the shadow of a boom mike cast on Lister and The Cat.

Star Trek: The Next Generation

Where No One Has Gone Before
Near the start of the episode, just as Riker says, 'you have all the time you need', the engine consultant stops and turns around. As he does so, a microphone can be seen above his head, hanging down. The camera quickly adjusts and it's not visible any more.

Conundrum
Just before encountering the Lysian destroyer the boom is visible in the top left of the screen very briefly.

Stargate SG-1

Children of the Gods (2)
When Daniel, Jack and Sam first meet the robed Jaffa in the woods, you can see the camera light in Daniel's glasses.

LET'S SWAP

This is a more specific brand of continuity mistake, occasionally caused by flipping the picture to make the action flow the right way, although that's mostly film-based. For TV shows, it's more often than not down to a mistaken second take – how often do you pay attention to what hand is being used to open a door?

Buffy the Vampire Slayer

Welcome to the Hellmouth (1)
While Giles is giving his speech about the Hellmouth the books he's holding keep changing from facing him to facing Buffy and back again.

The Wish
Xander stakes Angel and is thrown to Buffy's left, away from the machine. Seconds later as Buffy walks forwards, the angle changes to a shot where we see Xander fighting to her right, on the other side of the machine.

Near the start of the episode, in the scene where Cordelia is talking to the Cordettes and meets Anya, we see, during the close-ups of Harmony, that Anya is standing to camera right of the brunette Cordette, who is behind her. A few seconds later, in a longer shot, Anya is standing to camera left of the Cordette.

Dead Things
In the scene where Buffy, believing that she killed Warren's ex-girlfriend, is at the police station, the over-the-shoulder shot of the Desk Sergeant shows him holding the phone between his

shoulder and his ear. But in the front shot of him the phone has jumped to his hand.

Once More, with Feeling

Tara checks out Lethe's Bramble in the book at the Magic Box and, as she holds the sprig, she is facing to the left in the close-ups, but to the right in the long shots.

While Buffy is singing her song 'Something to Sing About' in the Bronze, she breaks a pool cue over a demon's head. She holds the remains in her right hand and clubs another demon in the face with it, then the camera cuts to another angle and it's now in her left hand as she uses it to stab the next demon.

Chosen

Buffy is giving her speech about being chosen and there is a shot of Andrew sitting on the couch next to Xander and Anya, but in several shots of the Potentials he can be seen standing on the other side of the room in front of the curtains. It's definitely him – his face isn't visible, but the clothes are exactly the same.

When Anya leads Andrew away to their station in the school, between shots she goes from having her right arm over his shoulders to having her left arm over his shoulders. She is off camera for a second, but not long enough to move to the opposite side of him and change hands.

Dawson's Creek

Future Tense

After Jack breaks his arm, the arm he has in a sling changes from left to right continually. It is especially noticeable when he is walking down the corridor at school.

Family Guy

From Method to Madness

When we first see the sign outside the Quahog institute of performing arts, it has a cartoon take on the comedy and tragedy masks in the corners. In the left-hand corner is a black mask with big ears and a smile, and on the right is a white mask with a frown. Later, the black mask has the frown and the white mask has the big ears and the smile; the third time you see the sign it has changed back again.

Fawlty Towers

A Touch of Class

When Basil brings in Lord Melbury's cases, they swap hands between the exterior and interior shots.

Friends

The One with the Butt

In the scene just before Joey goes into the shower, when he is thanking the director for the acting opportunity, the camera shots go back and forth between Joey and the director several times. During this series of shots, the parting in Joey's hair switches sides nearly every time. It appears that the entire shot is reversed – in the close-up, the shower curtain is on his left and the shadow to his right is sharply focused. In the lower (long) shot, the curtain is to his right, and the shadow on his left is more focused.

The One with the Dozen Lasagnes

Joey and Chandler buy a foosball table and Monica and Ross come over to play. They score as the blue team and are on the right-hand side of the table. When the credits are rolling, Monica is playing against Joey and Chandler again. She is on the left-hand side of the table but scores as the blue team again.

The One the Morning After

Immediately before Ross and Rachel storm in, the girls show Joey how much their waxing stuff hurts. Phoebe starts putting the wax on Joey's inner arm, but then the shot changes and she is spreading it on the outer side. Also, she slaps the strip on and the blue tab is hanging down off his arm, but then the shot changes again and it is on his arm with the other end of the strip hanging off the other side.

The One with a Chick. And a Duck.

When Ross is asking Joey and Chandler which suit he should wear for the TV thing the brown suit is in his right hand and the blue one is in his left hand. After Ross says 'really?' the shot changes to a wide view, and the two suits have changed places.

The One with Ross's Wedding, Part 2

As Ross says 'this is our wedding day', there is a close-up of Jack Gellar holding a bit of paper in his left hand (glasses in his other hand, out of shot). In the wide shot the paper is in his right hand, then jumps back to his left hand when the angle changes.

The One with the Proposal, Part 2

At the end of the episode when Chandler returns to his apartment, he opens the door, from the outside, with his right hand.

Then a cut to an inside view shows him opening it with his left hand on the handle.

The One with the Halloween Party
Phoebe is talking to Ursula's fiancé Eric as he is wiping sweat off his face with a napkin. He puts the napkin to his eye and then, in the next shot, it changes to the other eye without enough time having elapsed for him to change it. This happens again when at one point he's wiping his eye and then, on a change of shot, his forehead.

The One with Phoebe's Birthday Dinner
Rachel is telling Ross why she doesn't want to go to the dinner in celebration of Phoebe's birthday, and she says, 'the first sign is I don't want to, and . . . I'm not going'. While she says this, her left hand is completely empty, but then, in the next shot, the camera goes back to Ross and she can be seen holding the baby monitor in that hand. It then moves around in various shots afterwards.

The One with the Male Nanny
Towards the end of the episode, during a scene at Ross and Rachel's, Sandy picks up two puppets and puts one on each hand. He starts pulling the blue one onto his left hand, but when the angle changes there's a yellow one on his left hand, and a blue one on his right. There's a cut to Ross, then, when we go back to Sandy, the puppets have changed hands again.

Malcolm in the Middle

Long Drive
Malcolm's seat belt changes from on to off in the first scene with him and his mum in the car. When it's a shot from the front it's

on, but when it's a shot from the side (from the driver's side) you can see that the part of the seat belt that would be across Malcolm if it was on, is now behind him. This changes back and forth.

Monty Python's Flying Circus

Dinsdale

At the beginning of the 'Ministry of Silly Walks' sketch, John Cleese is holding his briefcase in his left hand. When the shot changes to the outside, showing him leaving the newsagents, it switches to his right.

Mr Bean

Mr Bean Goes to Town

Mr Bean places his shoe on top of the car at the back in the right-hand corner. But when he jumps out in front of the car, it is suddenly at the front in the middle.

Office, The

Downsize

After Gareth hits Tim on the head with his newspaper, the following shot shows that the briefcase and newspaper have swapped hands.

Red Dwarf

Thanks for the Memory

Lister's left foot and The Cat's left foot sustain injuries when they drop the gravestone; but The Cat is later seen to be wearing a plaster cast on his right foot.

Duct Soup
At the beginning of the episode, Kochanski is banging on the pipes with a spanner using her right hand. When the shot changes, she's using her left hand. There was no time for her to have changed hands between shots.

Seinfeld

The Boyfriend (1)
When George is lying on the floor in his underwear, a newspaper is on his right side. When they take the reverse shot (Jerry's view of him lying there), the newspaper is on George's left side.

Sex and the City

Ghost Town
Carrie, Samantha and Miranda are at the opening of Steve and Aidan's bar. Carrie lifts her hair off her neck with her right arm, but then, in the next shot, she is lowering her left arm.

Simpsons, The

Across whole show
On various occasions the front door, viewed from the inside of the house, has hinges – and therefore opens – on the wrong side, if you compare it to the shots of the door from the outside.

Krusty Gets Busted
Sideshow Bob is shouting and screaming just before he is taken away in a police van. Bart had been to Lisa's left but Lisa and Bart swap places right before Bart says 'take him away boys' so that Lisa is then to Bart's left.

There's No Disgrace Like Home
During the parts where you see the crowd applaud Mr Burns's speech there are two people on the bottom left of the screen who swap skin colour.

Homer Defined
When Smithers shows Mr Burns the picture of his dog, he is standing to the right of him. Immediately after, he is standing in front of the TV monitors.

I Married Marge
After Marge says she will marry Homer, at the beginning of the scene, the car is facing the power plant, and at the end, it is facing away from the plant.

Lisa's Pony
Homer enters the back left door of the auditorium. He has jumped to the right side when seen clapping.

Homer writes '4½ Reed' on his left shoe. When the owner of the music store asks him what Lisa plays, he is reading off his right shoe.

When Lisa calls Homer at work, Homer picks up the phone on his left side. Instantly, we see him hang the phone up on his right side.

Saturdays of Thunder
At the Institute, the clipboard Dave is holding repeatedly switches arms between shots. It also disappears entirely.

At the end of the episode, when Bart gets his trophy, Marge and Homer change positions between shots.

In the video store, Homer is carrying Maggie. Right after he picks up the tape, Maggie switches arms.

Separate Vocations

When Lisa enters the bad girls' washroom for the first time, the books she is carrying are first under one arm then the other.

In the cafeteria scene where Milhouse shoots a spitball at Kearney, in the shot after Milhouse says, 'We have order, but at what price', Milhouse, Lewis and the bullies have all changed positions at their tables.

A Star is Burns

Everybody is chanting 'Film Festival', and you can see that Mayor Quimby has his arm up. But in the next shot, in which you can see Marqe, he is holding up his other arm.

Homer the Great

When the Stonecutters are singing 'We do', the position of several characters, particularly the Martian and Chief Wiggum, change randomly as the camera angles change. The Martian starts at the end of the table on the right side, with Chief Wiggum two seats to the left of him. In later shots, first the Martian and then Wiggum are switched to the same position, midway up the left side. However, when the song ends, Wiggum has disappeared and the Martian remains in this new position.

Springfield Connection

Hans Moleman and Rev. Lovejoy are in the prison sitting to the far right of the bench (which is nearest to Homer's cell). In the next shot they are to the far left.

A Fish Called Selma

In the scene where Selma and Troy McClure get caught by the press outside the restaurant, Selma and Troy swap places between shots.

Bart After Dark

When the mob is at the gates of Belle's house, the door bell is first seen on the left-hand side of the gates. In the next shot (behind Flanders) it is in the centre of the gates.

The Old Man and the C Student

Homer offers Lenny some nuts and a spring pops out and gets Lenny in the left eye, but the next time we see Lenny the spring is in his right eye.

Today, I am a Klown

When we first see the medicine cabinet in the Simpson's bathroom the hinges are on the left. After Homer pokes it with the wire it opens as if the hinges are on the other side. The last time we see the cabinet, when Lisa rescues Maggie, the door is missing altogether.

Smallville

Perry

At the end of the episode, Perry and Clark arrive at the intersection to wait for the bus. They walk out into the intersecting road, and the bus arrives, and takes a position in the middle of the road, since they are standing in the right-hand lane. Perry and Clark say their goodbyes, and a further shot of the bus from behind shows that it is in the right-hand lane as it starts up ready to move from the stop.

South Park

Osama Bin Laden Has Farty Pants

When Osama is videotaping his message, Kenny is sitting on the left-hand chair, but when you see the video on the news, Kenny is sitting on the far right chair next to the goat.

WE'LL WEATHER THE WEATHER

Much to the chagrin of directors everywhere, the weather *still* can't be controlled. Not so much of a problem for TV shows, which are by and large based indoors, but even then they can't always make it do what they want . . .

Frasier

Space Quest

Frasier (and later the others) come back to his apartment to avoid the rain – they shake off umbrellas, and we even hear the storm at the very start of the scene. However, there's no rain on the balcony and it can't be covered, as we see in 'Call Me Irresponsible', during the 'obligatory sex scene', that when it's raining the balcony gets soaked.

M*A*S*H

Bug Out (60 mins.)

The chopper carrying the soldier with the wounded back takes off into a cloudy sky and, even accounting for the poor quality of the film, the weather looks very dull. The shot changes to show Radar, Hawkeye and Margaret watching the chopper leave in bright sunshine.

Simpsons, The

Bart Gets an F

When Bart hands Ms Krabappel his final test, there are some shots going back and forth between their faces. During the first shot (looking at Ms Krabbappel), you can see a window behind her and, outside the window, there is no snow, even though there was a whole lot of it the day before. In the next shot, the snow *is* there. As the camera goes back and forth, the snow disappears and reappears.

GIVING THE GAME AWAY

We all *know* that TV programmes aren't really real, and that every special effect or stunt is carefully planned, but that doesn't mean we like being dragged out of our suspension of disbelief and have brutal reality shoved in our faces. These mistakes are all the kind of thing which can deliver just such an unpleasant jolt . . .

Alias

Truth Be Told

When Syd's dad rescues her in the car park, he starts shooting at the other car. After firing one shot the slide of his gun locks back (indicating it's out of bullets), but when the angle changes he carries on firing without reloading.

Double Agent

Sydney and Vaughn are at Sydney's apartment, cooking dinner. Sydney reaches into the supposedly hot oven, without an oven mitt on, and doesn't seem to have any problems with the heat.

Angel

Lonely Hearts

In the scene where Angel runs after the barman, towards the end (after the barman has tried to pass on the demon to Kate and Angel stopped him), there is a mirror, and when Angel runs past it he has a reflection (vampires are not supposed to have reflections).

The Prodigal
In the scene where Kate finds her father dead in his apartment, just after the shot of the vampire bites in his neck, she is sitting over him and you can see her father blinking a few times.

To Shanshu in L.A.
As Angel is pulling out of the parking lot to follow the W&H Trucks, you can see his reflection in his rear view mirror. In some episodes the rear view mirror is removed, probably to avoid this mistake.

Disharmony
At the very end, as Angel walks out of the door his reflection is seen in the panes of glass on the door.

When Harmony spills her pig's blood on the keyboard, the computer shorts out and the monitor flickers off, but the mouse cursor is still visible, showing the shortinq effect was just that, an effect, because the computer's still working fine.

Ground State
As Gwen is walking towards the lift in Irwin's building you can see Angel's reflection on the shiny door.

The Cautionary Tale of Numero Cinco
When the mysterious person hands Cinco the business card during the 50s flashback (in the restaurant where he is sitting waiting for business), it says, 'Wolfram & Hart, Attorney's at Law'. Clearly, there should be no apostrophe in 'Attorneys' – not a mistake a professional law firm would make.

Are You Being Served?

The Punch and Judy Affair

The staff are assembled in Mr Rumbold's office with the exception of Mr Lucas, who comes rushing in late. However, just before he does you can see him standing outside the door, waiting for his cue to rush in.

Band of Brothers

Replacements

In the shot before Buck falls back he fires twice. The first time everything looks normal, but the second time the cocking bolt on the side of his Thompson doesn't move.

Black Adder

The Black Seal

At the end of the episode, all the main characters are drinking poisoned wine. When they have drunk the wine, everybody falls over. When they show Blackadder, one of the men lifts his head up. He's supposed to be dead.

Beer

When Edmund leaves Melchett's house to prepare for the evening, he walks away and bumps into the wall, causing it to wobble.

Duel and Duality

At the end of the episode, when Blackadder is talking to the king, you see Hugh Laurie (Prince Regent) moving his hand up and scratching his head when he's meant to be dead.

Nob and Nobility
After Blackadder accidentally kills Smedly with one of the suicide pills, he starts ranting about how useless Smedly is as a hero, because he was dumb enough to fall for the old 'poisoned cup routine'. As he does so, you can see the supposedly dead Smedly behind him, still breathing normally.

Buffy the Vampire Slayer

Nightmares
The Master's artificial thumbnail is visibly falling off in a few shots of the opening teaser.

Halloween
When everyone is turned into his or her costume, Willow is turned into a ghost. Throughout the entire episode, she can't touch anything (can't turn the pages of a book, etc.), yet towards the end when she and Giles go to Ethan's shop, and she leaves, the bell on the door rings, showing that she opened and closed the door, even though she can walk through walls and can't actually touch the door. The curtain moves when she leaves too.

I Only Have Eyes for You
During the flashbacks to 1955 James and Grace dance, and James later shoots himself, to the song 'I Only Have Eyes for You', which wasn't released until 1959.

When She Was Bad
Willow, Cordy, Miss Calendar and Giles are wheeled over the bones of the Master. When Giles goes past, his hand brushes against the bones and the skeleton bends, revealing that it is in fact rubber.

Anne

During the fight scene at the end when Buffy is fighting the demons you see her throw one of the demons off the platform. If you watch him fall you can see him land safely on a conveniently placed mat.

When Buffy runs in front of the car you can see that she is wearing knee pads. You have to look quite closely because they are the same colour as her tights.

Faith, Hope and Trick

During Faith's fight outside the Bronze, when she stakes the vampire, watch carefully and you will see the rubber stake bending under the force of the impact. That's not going to kill anything.

Revelations

When Buffy and Faith are fighting, the kick Faith aims at Buffy's face right after she says, 'We can work this out', very noticeably misses, but Buffy still reacts as though it landed with normal force.

The Initiative

Several times during Spike's escape from the Initiative, his reflection can be seen in the glass. Vampires aren't supposed to have reflections.

Wild at Heart

Towards the end when Willow is in the science lab casting her spell you can see the wires that are used to levitate the vials. They are especially noticeable after the vials drop and they are left dangling.

Crush
At the start, when the porter is dragged back onto the train, you can see (more obviously if you watch in slow motion) that there's absolutely nothing grabbing him, not even someone's shadow.

All the Way
In one fight scene, Buffy uses a car door to block a kick from a vampire. The window of the car breaks before the kick connects with it. In fact, it breaks while the foot is still in midair.

Gone
When Buffy is invisible and in the social office, she is searching for the summer files, and a thumb is seen picking them up.

Older and Far Away
Spike follows Buffy into the hallway right by her front door, next to which is a mirror. In this mirror we see Spike's reflection. Vampires do not have reflections, so Spike should not have been visible.

Two to Go (1)
In the opening of the episode, Willow has gone crazy and is trying to kill the two remaining members of the Trio, so she is pulling the wall of the jail apart brick by brick. The problem is that if you look carefully, they are obviously not bricks being pulled away; they look more like plastic or plaster.

Chosen
Anya beheads two Ubervamps. The second time she swings the sword it very noticeably doesn't go anywhere near the Ubervamp's neck, but is closer to its stomach. The head comes off anyway.

Charmed

Sleuthing with the Enemy
When Phoebe throws the potion at Cole's coat, the vial doesn't shatter, even though it sounds like it. Watch closely, and you'll see the purple, unbroken vial bounce off the coat and away out of shot without any of the potion touching the coat.

Witches in Tights
After the girls realise that removing their masks alters their way of thinking, The Aggressor dashes in and uses his power to throw Phoebe across the room. After this, Piper runs to Phoebe and screams 'Lyssie' (the nickname the cast and crew uses for Alyssa Milano, who plays Phoebe).

CSI: Crime Scene Investigation

Pledging Mr Johnson
While the morgue's examiner opens Johnson's right eye with his fingers, the 'corpse's' eyelid twitches repeatedly.

CSI: Miami

Entrance Wound
While Horatio and Alexx are examining the prostitute's body, you can see the corpse breathe in a side view.

Dawson's Creek

Pilot
In the scene after school when Dawson cycles up beside Joey to

ask her to go to the cinema with him, Jen and Pacey, he's begging her to go but by mistake calls her Jen instead of Joey.

All Good Things . . . (1)
When Doug pulls Jack over at the start of this episode, listen closely as Jack says 'It's a deserted road.' You can hear the sound of a car passing in the background. Not very deserted then.

EastEnders

In the episode aired on 12 December 2003, in the laundrette a shelf has fallen off the wall and Dot Cotton needs someone to fix it. The wall is clearly false, as every time Dot touches the shelf, the wall wobbles. Later the same episode Martin Fowler fixes the shelf and says something like 'the wall will fall down before the shelf does' – very true

Farscape

A Human Reaction
As John and Aeryn are walking up to the safe house you can see make-up mixed in with the rain dripping off John's nose.

Fawlty Towers

Across whole show
Whenever somebody closes a door, leans against a wall, or goes up/down the stairs and brushes against the wall, it wobbles, revealing that the walls are lightweight stand-up props.

The Germans
When Basil is turning the fire alarm on and off, he puts the key

next to the red box and turns it. However, there isn't a slot for the key to actually go in; he's just holding it close and turning it.

The Kipper and the Corpse

Basil, Manuel and Polly are trying to hide Mr Leeman from the other guests, so they put him in a cupboard. While they are talking to the people staying in the room, Mr Leeman's hand comes out of the cupboard. Watch carefully, and you can see the actor opening the door from the inside, and then putting his arm down, making him look like the corpse.

Friends

Across whole show

Any scenes outside Central Perk always sound as if they're on a set (which, let's be honest, they are) – the sound is often muted and footsteps on the pavement have a very slight echo to them.

The One with the Butt

This is the episode where Joey is doubling Al Pacino's butt and his shadow is clearly visible when he's shooting the scene in the shower – he's wearing boxer shorts.

The One with Two Parts: Part 2

Dr Mitchell (George Clooney) answers the phone (while Monica and Rachel are pretending to be each other), and starts handing the phone to Rachel, saying 'Rachel, it's your dad', but he should be passing it to Monica (as he thinks her name is Rachel). The angle then changes, and now he's handing it to Monica.

The One with the Flashback

When Monica offers Joey lemonade he misunderstands and he

takes off his clothes behind the lamp; the tops of his boxer shorts are clearly visible when he realises that Monica was only offering lemonade.

Phoebe and Ross are in the soon-to-be-closed bar sitting on the pool table. He clears it of everything, but a few seconds later he stops making out because the 'damn balls are in the way' and he somehow magicks up a handful of snooker balls. If you look closely when he's clearing the table, there are two dark balls at the side which he studiously ignores, and which Phoebe then surreptitiously grabs and takes onto the table with her so Ross can grab them later.

The One with the Giant Poking Device

The giant poking device is supposedly long enough to reach right the way across to the next building, but on at least one occasion when they're holding it, you see the end bob up at the bottom of the screen right in front of them.

The One where They're Going to PARTY!

When Monica and Phoebe are in Central Perk, Phoebe is looking through the list of ideas that Monica has come up with for the use of Phoebe's van. Look closely (most obvious just after Phoebe says 'let's plan the wedding reception') and you can see that every single page of the notebook Phoebe is holding has the same thing written on it, instead of lots of different ideas that Monica is meant to have had.

The One with Joey's Dirty Day

After Joey is caught in Charlton Heston's shower, he wraps a towel around his waist and sits on the arm of the chair. The line of the Speedo underwear is visible under the towel.

The One with Ross's Wedding, Part 2
Joey is talking on a cell phone with Phoebe as he walks down the aisle. He holds the phone out to Ross saying 'it's Phoebe', and one can clearly see that the phone's screen is completely blank. The phone isn't even turned on.

The One with the Ballroom Dancing
Right at the end of the episode, Phoebe's got a job interview. We see the outside of a massage parlour, but the name on the awning has been superimposed – it moves about a bit while the shot itself is still.

The One with All the Thanksgivings
When Joey has the turkey on his head, and Chandler is by the door, look at the wall to Chandler's right. It's a 'wild wall', – i.e. a movable wall put there to extend the set outwards an additional few feet, since the camera normally doesn't see that far forward. The wall angles oddly away from the room, and you can see how the line and pattern of the hallway floor continues into the room.

The One with Rachel's Inadvertent Kiss
When Ross is sitting on the sofa doing his 'Watching TV' bit, there is a brief shot of the blank screen that he is pretending to watch. The screen reflects the fact that the sofa is empty.

The One with Chandler's Dad
When the Porsche is first seen, there are smear marks on the bonnet from previous takes of Ross diving across it.

The One with the Engagement Picture
If you pause the shot of the paper which shows the picture of

Monica and Joey, can see that the announcement written there starts out fine, but near the end the middle part is repeated again.

The One After 'I do'

In this episode – the one after Monica and Chandler get married – Chandler says he can't dance because his shoes are slippery. But a close look reveals that the reason he slipped was because he stood on the bottom of Monica's dress, not because of the shoes.

The One in Massapequa

At Ross and Monica's parents' 35th wedding anniversary, when the parents are talking to Ross and Rachel, there is a picture of the parents in the background, in exactly the same location, wearing exactly the same clothes. That photo would have had to be taken, printed and blown up no more than an hour before the events depicted.

Home Improvement

Across whole show

Anytime the kids are shown running through the back yard, it is very obvious from the sound that they are running on a wooden set floor instead of grass-covered ground.

M*A*S*H

Major Fred C Dobbs

When Frank is digging for gold, he has two shadows, caused by the artificial lighting used during filming.

5 O'Clock Charlie
Charlie drops the bomb on the General's jeep but it is obvious that the jeep is already burned and mangled when the explosion starts.

Operation Noselift
Henry is trying to convince Baker how wonderful the camp is; he says that they 'had both *The Thing* and *The Blob* in one week'. *The Blob* was made in 1958. This season of *M*A*S*H* is set in 1951 and 1952 (and the Korean War ended in 1953 anyway).

When Baker is talking with Father Mulcahy it is clear that Baker's nose is prosthetic. The colour doesn't match as well as it does in other scenes.

The Incubator
Col. Lambert tells Hawkeye and Trapper that with enough notice he could get them anything, even a B-52. The first B-52A entered service in 1954, a year after the Korean War ended.

Bug Out (60 mins.)
When Col. Potter is in the helicopter looking for a new site for the camp, you can see landscape reflecting in the canopy. This never changes position although they're meant to be flying around.

End Run
In the mess, it is noticeable that everyone has their food on metal trays and ceramic dishes. Sgt Zale, though, has his lemon pie in a polystyrene dish – so that it doesn't hurt Klinger when he gets it in the face.

Malcolm in the Middle

Pilot

At the start of the pilot, when Lois tells Hal to raise his arms so she can shave his armpits, look at the bottom of the screen and you will briefly see that Hal is wearing something to cover up his privates.

Forwards Backwards

Malcolm scares Reese with the horn while Reese is in the shower; Reese falls and we get a glimpse of the shorts he is wearing. Shorts in the shower?

Zoo

When the tarantula is put on Hal at the zoo, the shot is of a yellow shirt only, with the tarantula crawling on it. When the shot changes to where the whole Hal is seen, it is easy to tell that the tarantula is fake – it is larger than it was and is in a different spot on Hal's shirt.

Neighbours

Across whole show

At the time Nina was receiving text messages from Taj, her phone used to ring when she got a text, but sometimes it made a text-alert noise. She also read one of the messages before it came on the screen (the shot was of the screen).

Nina first wrote 'Born to Try', the song which was being released by Delta Goodrem (the actress who plays her), to go along with the show. She then somehow managed to just 'improvise' the tune and words to her (Delta's) third single 'Innocent Eyes'. What a handy coincidence.

Only Fools and Horses

Who's a Pretty Boy?
When Denzil's wife storms out of the room and slams the door behind her, the wall to the right of the door lurches forward under the pressure of the closing door.

Quantum Leap

Across whole show
For those not familiar with the show, a scientist named Sam leaps into people's bodies and changes their futures. The viewers see the person as Sam, but characters in the show still see the person Sam has leapt into. So when Sam leaps into a child or a short person, the other characters should, technically, be looking at Sam's chest when they are trying to look him in the eyes because that's where their eyes would be. Instead, they always look right into Sam's eyes – too high if you are really talking to a child or short person.

Red Dwarf

Me2
Lister is taking the painting to the room belonging to the two Rimmers; he stops outside the door and says, 'Second Technician Arnold J Rimmer and Second Technician Arnold J Rimmer'. He then presses the pad to open the door. Watch carefully, as the door opens before he touches the pad.

Backwards
Most of the things that happen on 'Backwards Earth' in this episode are correct, except, of course, in reverse. But there is an exception: in the scene in the café, when the waitress comes to 'dirty' the table, she tips a box of trash on it. If you play this scene backwards, the trash leaps from the table into the box. Even on a 'backwards earth' I can't believe that trash spontaneously leaps about.

Bodyswap
When Kryten takes the syringe out of Lister's head, the needle doesn't come out of the syringe properly, so Kryten puts his hand in front of the needle to try and hide the mistake.

Meltdown
Some of the episode must have been filmed on a cold day – you can see Rimmer's breath condensing in the cold air. But Rimmer is a hologram – and holograms don't breathe (because they don't need to).

Seinfeld

The Suicide
In this episode when Jerry leaves his room to talk to his neighbour about their fight, he shuts his door and the wall shakes – either that's a giveaway about the set, or that's one unsturdy apartment . . .

Sex and the City

The Big Journey
When Carrie and Samantha go to San Francisco there is a scene

where Samantha is in the bath. She stands up and her front is covered in bubbles. When she gets out of the bath it is clear from the mirror behind her that she is wearing a red bra and knicker set. It's especially strange that she's covering up for this scene when viewers have seen much more of her than her backside in the past.

Simpsons, The

Lisa's Pony

As Homer falls asleep in the car, he hits the dashboard with his fist, and the airbag pops out. If you watch in slow motion though, he doesn't hit anything at all.

Saturdays of Thunder

On his soapbox derby racer, Bart is pounding his hammer on an area that doesn't have nails in it.

Bart Gets Famous

When Snake is holding a gun up to Apu, Apu hits the alarm. The only problem is that as there is no button to press, he hits the counter.

Bart vs. Australia

While Bart is trying to make the toilet water flow the other way, in one of the flushes the toilet begins to dispense water before Bart pulls the chain.

It's a Mad, Mad, Mad, Mad Marge

When the kids are holding the video cameras, there are no straps to keep their hands on the cameras, so it looks like their hands are glued to the sides.

Smallville

Across whole show

There are times when it is quite evident that Michael Rosenbaum is voluntarily bald i.e. shaven.

Some Mothers do 'Ave 'Em

Moving House

At the beginning of the episode when Frank is directing the vans, one gets its windscreen broken by a ladder from another van. However, the glass breaks just before the ladder touches it.

Star Trek: Deep Space Nine

The Passenger

When the Koblian officer opens Vantika's eyes to run a retinal scan, his pupils dilate, despite the fact that he is dead.

Star Trek: The Next Generation

Skin of Evil

Immediately after Commander Riker gets pulled into the sludge-type black substance, watch the left side of the screen. When the away team looks into it, after Riker's face comes out of the sludge, you will see something plop into the goo; it is Geordi's phaser falling out of his holster when he leaned over the pool of goo.

West Wing, The

The Stackhouse Filibuster

When Josh is at his computer in front of a part-written email, as Donna asks, 'What are you doing?' he taps a few keys, at most ten, and two new paragraphs appear on the screen.

X-Files, The

Musings of a Cigarette-Smoking Man

When the cigarette-smoking man is writing his letter of resignation on his typewriter, it is apparent that the letters are already there – he is simply typing over them.

BLOOD STAINED

Many TV shows feature wounds, spillages and other random dribbles, whether during a fight or a slapstick moment. But the necessity of multiple takes can mean that no matter how careful you are, that custard pie will never hit the same way twice . . .

Black Adder

Beer
Edmund throws his drink into the cupboard under the stairs, where it leaves a stain on the floor. Yet when he directs Queenie there a few seconds later, the floor is unstained.

Buffy the Vampire Slayer

Phases
When Willow is running from the werewolf she falls and gets a big mud stain on her trousers. In the next shot, when she gets up, it has disappeared.

Graduation Day (1)
In the scene where Giles stabs the Mayor and he takes the foil out of his chest, matter from the wound is visible on his shirt. When the shot changes to another angle it has completely disappeared. It has been established that the Mayor is invincible and his wounds can heal quickly, but it still takes a second or two for his wounds to close up, they don't just disappear.

Fool for Love
When Riley is dressing Buffy's wound, it is much further to the

left side of where she was actually staked, which was more central on her stomach.

The Weight of the World
Glory challenges Dawn to name one person who can cope with life on earth, and we see a close-up of Dawn answering 'Buffy'. In this shot, the black mark (where she has been anointed) that was there in the previous shot and the one after, has completely disappeared.

Tough Love
Glory crushes Tara's hand causing her blood to drip onto the bench. In later shots, however, there is no blood on the bench.

Gone
Willow is spraying the invisible traffic cone, but she only sprays a little bit before leaving to track down the van. When Xander shows Anya the cone later on it's completely coloured.

Grave (2)
During the opening of the episode, Willow's nose starts bleeding and she gets blood on her upper lip. Over the next few shots the blood consistently keeps appearing and disappearing.

Once More, with Feeling
During the opening song, Buffy stabs a demon with a sword. She then walks across to the hostage and cuts him free, but when we see the sword there isn't any blood, despite the fact that seconds ago there was a demon impaled on it.

Chosen
Buffy gets stabbed by an Ubervamp. In one scene blood is

running down her shirt but in the final scene she walks towards where Sunnydale had been and her shirt is clean.

Same Time, Same Place
Gnarl cuts Dawn across the stomach, paralysing her and ripping her shirt, but when Buffy and Xander are carrying her home there is no tear in her shirt nor any blood. Also, when Buffy goes back to kill Gnarl, he tears her shirt but seconds later the rip has gone.

Friends

The One After the Superbowl, Part 1
When Brooke Shields is throwing water at Joey, he gets a large spot of water on his shirt. As the scene continues the size of this water mark often changes.

The One where No One's Ready
While Joey and Chandler are arguing about the chair Phoebe gets houmous on her dress, but in some scenes the stain is much smaller than in others.

The One with the Inappropriate Sister
After talking about hammer darts, Joey puts his hand through the wall next to the fridge, then in the next scene the hole is gone. It is possible that it was fixed, but since it is on the same day, and there's not a mark to be seen, I doubt It.

M*A*S*H

Dear Dad, Again
When Frank is getting drunk he spills gin down the front of his

vest. A few shots later, just before he collapses, it suddenly dries out significantly.

Requiem for a Lightweight
In the first shot of Trapper running behind the Jeep, he has a large patch of sweat on his chest. For the rest of the scene it is dry.

Divided We Stand
Margaret is shampooing Frank's hair; she raises her foam-covered hands to allow him to kiss her. The camera angle changes and her hands are nearly foam-free.

For the Good of the Outfit
Frank is shaving; when he bends down to pick up the envelope containing shrapnel fragments, the foam on his face and ear suddenly dries up. The shot must have needed a lot of takes.

A Full Rich Day
The mud spots on Lt Smith's face change from scene to scene.

Alcoholics Unanimous
During the scene which culminates in Frank declaring the camp dry, the patches of water on his helmet change position.

Of Moose and Men
After Hawkeye and Burns drive through the puddle, the mud shown on the colonel's face is different in the long and close-up shots.

Smilin' Jack
After Jack delivers the patient to the MASH, he is taking photos

of the operation and there is no wound on the patient's right hand. It only appears when Col. Potter says that he treated it 'months ago'.

The Kids

When Margaret pins Frank's Purple Heart on, his scrubs are very damp with sweat. When he enters the swamp, they're practically dry.

Welcome to Korea (60 mins.)

During the shelling on the road, BJ gets very muddy. But when they get to the bar all the mud has disappeared from his right arm and he is much cleaner.

Simpsons, The

Saturdays of Thunder

Nelson makes a hole in the Honor Roller during the finals. This hole disappears and reappears between shots.

Bart Gets Famous

When Bart is copying from the books in the kitchen, he is seen writing on the paper. In the next shot of him, the paper is clean.

Homie the Clown

Homer is driving home in a bad mood (just before he gets stopped by Chief Wiggum) and you can see that there is a pattern on the side of the car. In the next shot when Wiggum is walking alongside the car there is no pattern.

Lemon of Troy

After Bart attempts to escape by using spray-paint cans as

rockets, his feet alternate between clean and spray-painted for a few shots.

Lisa's Date with Density

When Jimbo and Co are 'coleslawing' Skinner's house, he wakes up when coleslaw hits his window. When the scene moves outside, there isn't any coleslaw on any of the windows.

Bye Bye Nerdy

There are two problems with Lisa's Indian burns. When we first see them, she has four burns. Then, while she is showing them to the bullies, there are three, then four again. Finally, in the very next scene when she is walking with Nelson in the schoolyard, they are gone altogether.

Worst Episode Ever

During Tom Savini's presentation, the comic-book seller eats a kind of cookie. Fake blood then starts to flow from his mouth and he takes his T-shirt to wipe it. There are no stains on the T-shirt after that.

South Park

An Elephant Makes Love to a Pig

Kyle has a black eye, but it has magically disappeared by the time he gets home.

Pink Eye

When we see Kenny from the front, the hole in his head exposing his brain appears on his left side, but in the shot revealing the top of his head, when he is biting people, the hole is in the back of his head.

Stargate SG-1

Enigma

After Jack first tells Daniel to dial home, he brushes off the edge of the Dial Home Device (DHD), which is covered with about two inches of ash, but when we see the DHD in the background just seconds later, it has only a light dusting of ash on it.

TIME FOR A CHANGE

Time constantly marches on, even when you're taking a break from filming, and unless you pay attention to the clocks, they can tell an unwanted story about just how long a certain scene took to shoot . . .

24

10:00 P.M.–11:00 P.M.

The terrorists give Jack a telephone and ask him to kill the senator and then they'll tell him where Kim is. They tell him they'll ring that phone at exactly 10.45 p.m. When Jack gets to the senator's suites it's around 10.20 p.m., and the terrorists telephone shortly after he arrives. For all they know he could still be en route to the hotel so why were they so quick off the mark?

1:00 A.M.–2:00 A.M.

Shortly after the clock display reads 01.44, the time is shown again . . . and it's 01.42.

3:00 A.M.–4:00 A.M.

The show claims to be in real time, and although those viewers who aren't too eagle-eyed will argue that it is, there is undisputed evidence in this episode that it isn't accurate. After the final ad break, the clock reads 03.52. At least two minutes later, when we see Teri and 'Alan York' turn a corner in their car, the clock is displayed at the bottom of the screen, and it is still 03.52. The same sort of thing happens earlier in the episode, when there is a good ten minutes or so between the clock showing 03.26 and then 03.30.

Buffy the Vampire Slayer

Beauty and the Beasts

Buffy has to see the school psychiatrist but she finds him dead in his office. As she walks into his office she says she's on time for her two o'clock appointment, but the clock over the office door reads twenty past four.

Frasier

Across whole show

Frasier claims to have been 'punched in the face yesterday by a man now dead'. When he says this, two nights have passed since the murder. The next day Niles panics at the café and then sleeps for twenty hours. This time Frasier claims he was punched in the face three days previously by a man now dead, when it has been at least four days.

Futurama

Xmas Story

Fry looks up at the clock tower and sees that the display reads '04.26', which implies it is four in the morning, instead of four in the afternoon as it should be. In addition, once he has climbed to the top of the tower, the clock has no '0' before the time and simply reads '4.26'. The zero returns right at the end of the episode, in a wide shot of New New York.

Monty Python's Flying Circus

Oh, You're No Fun Anymore

During the science-fiction sketch, when Eric Idle is reporting his blancmange sighting to John Cleese, the clock in the background jumps backwards a few minutes.

Sex and Violence
The sketch is tracking the history of the Funniest Joke in the World. We are told that the Germans developed their version of the joke in the autumn of 1944 but the caption on the screen says 1942.

Simpsons, The

Bart the Murderer
At the beginning of the episode, watch the clock as Homer walks in – the time changes between shots.

Like Father, Like Klown
In Lovejoy's office, the clock on the wall keeps changing the time.

When Krusty arrives at the Simpson house, the time on the clock in the background changes.

Lisa's Pony
In the kitchen, there is a clock on the wall that suddenly appears, changes sides of the room, and changes times.

Separate Vocations
When Lisa is clapping erasers because she sassed Miss Hoover a second time, the room's clock is visible near the top of the ceiling. However, the clock wasn't there several shots earlier.

Sweet Seymour Skinner's Baadasssss Song
As Marge, Bart and Lisa are watching the videos at the beginning of the episode, the clock changes from one time to another between shots.

SUSTENANCE FOR THE SOUL

Another side effect of editing – people may say 'never work with animals or children' – but most continuity supervisors would probably rather have eating banned in everything ever filmed. . .

Angel

To Shanshu In L.A.

While Wes is lecturing Cordelia on wants and desires, the number of bites taken from the doughnut changes; in one instance it breaks in half, most visibly when Wes takes a bite from Cordy's doughnut on the angle change. It then somehow repairs itself.

Band of Brothers

Crossroads

In the scene where the men are in the barn, Luz is eating. In one shot he is chewing and moving his mouth (with the appropriate sounds), but, in the next shot, his mouth isn't moving at all, yet the chewing sound is still audible.

Boy Meets World

A Very Topanga Christmas

When Topanga tries the eggnog, you can tell that there is nothing in the paper cup, but she still 'drinks' it with no problems.

Poetic Licence: An Ode to Holden Caulfield

When Jack, Rachel and Eric are studying, Jack eats half of his apple, then the three argue, but when it cuts back to Jack eating his apple again, it is now whole and untouched.

Buffy the Vampire Slayer

Once More, with Feeling
From the start of the second scene in the Magic Box (the one with the songs 'I've Got a Theory', 'Bunnies' and 'What Can't We Face?'), the doughnut and cruller on Xander's plate constantly switch places.

Curb Your Enthusiasm

The Benadryl Brownie
When everyone is in Larry's house, sitting in the TV room eating brownies, the number of brownies on the plate changes between shots.

Dawson's Creek

Love Bites
When Jen is talking to Grams and pours herself a glass of juice the fridge behind her is open. The camera cuts to Grams and when it cuts back the fridge is closed and the jug of juice has disappeared. While the camera does leave Jen for a few seconds, it was nowhere near long enough to put the juice back in the fridge and close it, then run back to where she was standing. Also, there's no sound of the fridge door closing.

Ellen

The Puppy Episode (1)
Ellen tells her friends that she is gay and then starts to digress.

There are some wine glasses on the counter directly behind her. In several shots of the friends around the table, there are no glasses to be seen, but when Audrey says, 'I thought you had something important to tell us', she is holding a glass of wine. When Ellen is next seen, the glasses are no longer on the counter, and they actually appear on the coffee table a moment later when the friends get up to leave. Yet no one actually served the wine or got up to get any from the counter.

Family Guy

He's Too Sexy for His Fat

In the scene where Stewie is eating chocolate cake, he shoves his head in it and covers himself in cake. However, when Peter walks in after having lipo, all the cake is gone and Stewie is completely clean.

Fawlty Towers

The Builders

Polly brings Mr O'Reilly a cup of tea and it is obvious on several occasions that there is nothing in the cup. Not only does he hold it in such a way that you can see inside, but when Basil snatches it away nothing spills out.

Basil the Rat

While Basil and Sybil are talking to the public health inspector in the kitchen (on his second visit), Basil breaks two bottles of wine. When he removes the second bottle, there are two bottles remaining on the rack, but when the camera cuts away and then back when he breaks the bottle, there is only one bottle left on the rack.

Frasier

The Last Time I Saw Maris

Niles, who is drunk in Frasier's apartment, puts a six-pack of beer cans on the table by Martin's chair. The pack rotates on the table between shots, going from a horizontal to a vertical position and back at least once.

Friends

The One with Mrs Bing

When they are eating at the restaurant with Chandler's mum, Rachel is feeding Paolo out of her hand. The piece of food is gone as he licks her hand but returns when Rachel takes her hand away from his mouth.

Again, while they are all eating at the restaurant, and Mrs Bing is telling Rachel how to write a book, the size and position of the tortilla on Rachel's plate changes between shots without her touching it.

The One with the List

Ross, Joey and Chandler are in Chandler and Joey's apartment talking about Ross's decision between Julie and Rachel. Chandler has a green bottle in his hand. He puts it down behind the computer by the microwave. When Ross starts listing Rachel's 'cons' the bottle is at the opposite end of the counter.

The One where Ross and Rachel Take a Break

When Monica and Phoebe are eating with the diplomat and his translator, watch the translator's chocolate cake. It either rotates, has some taken out of it, or is a different piece. Whichever it is, the cake changes size, shape or position without him ever touching it.

The One After Ross Says Rachel
At Ross's disastrous wedding reception, Monica and Chandler are piling their dinner plates with food while arranging to meet for a second 'encounter'. Chandler's plate is stacked with various foods when he agrees to meet Monica in the cellar. He tosses his plate back on the table to rush off without eating anything, but the plate is, miraculously, nearly empty.

The One with Joey's New Brain
Joey is talking to the woman whose brain he receives in *Days of Our Lives*. As the shot changes she is holding a glass, then a cigarette, then a glass again, with no time to change from one to the other, let alone find a place to put the discarded item.

The One in Massapequa
Jack Gellar is eating food off a stick. When he finishes he holds the stick while Rachel asks him if he has any pearls of wisdom. We can see the stick over Judy's shoulder. In the next shot the stick is gone from his hand, then we see Judy put it down on a table, then it reappears in his hand, before disappearing for good.

The One with the Halloween Party
Rachel returns from running after the boy that she told to 'shut up', and Joey is seen picking up a piece of food, sniffing it and making a face and then putting it back on the tray. However, in the next shot, without moving, Joey is munching on something – he didn't have anything in his hand before.

The One in Barbados, Part 2

When Ross and Charlie are hiding from the other scientists, behind the plant, the drinks they are holding refill themselves and Charlie's ornament in her drink keeps switching to different sides of the glass.

The One with the Male Nanny

Near the end of the episode Ross gets a beer while he is arguing with Rachel as to whether they should fire the overly sensitive male nanny. Between shots the label on the bottle moves around.

The One with the Mugging

Joey visits Monica and Chandler's apartment. He gets something to drink from the fridge to keep his bladder full for the audition. When he closes the fridge he has two bottles in his left hand. The camera cuts to Monica, then back to Joey. He still has two cans in his left hand but he is holding them differently.

Futurama

A Big Piece of Garbage

In the scene where Leela is telling Fry how even his food is recycled (just after they have seen the video of the origin of the garbage-ball), Fry's drink can and sandwich can be seen on the table. After the close-up of Fry his sandwich has disappeared but, in the next full-table shot, it's back (albeit moved to Fry's right along with his drink can).

A Flight to Remember

The food cart completely disappears once LaBarbara stops playing the things on it like a drumkit.

My Problem with Popplers
'Ape Leela' 's salt falls off her head and then half of it reappears and falls off again as Lrr is picking her up.

M*A*S*H

Edwina
As Hawkeye and Eddie are going to sit down for lunch, on the table is ketchup, a bowl, pepper and salt. The shot switches to them sat down and the order is now bowl, ketchup, salt and pepper.

Sticky Wicket
At lunch, when Frank is getting his own back against Hawkeye, in the long shots of the table the plate of bread is beside Henry and in the close-ups it is in front of Trapper.

The Ringbanger
We see Radar outside Col. Brighton's tent with a glass of milk to slip into the tent. Before he does so, the camera switches to the inside of the tent and, if you look at the bottom left corner of the screen, you'll see the milk is already there.

Private Charles Lamb
In some shots the Spam lamb has mashed potato eyes and a carrot mouth, in others it has green eyes and no obvious mouth.

Soldier of the Month
Radar gets his breakfast and is given a large dollop of mashed potatoes. When he sits down to eat, the potatoes are gone and there is something unidentifiable in their place.

End Run
When BJ tells Hawkeye not to forget his old friends, the level of gin in BJ's glass has risen.

Margaret's Engagement
When Margaret arrives from Tokyo, BJ and Hawkeye's squashed orange disappears from the ground.

Malcolm in the Middle

Across whole show
It is Dewey's birthday and Malcolm grabs a piece of the cake. There's a shot of Dewey followed by one of Malcolm, who is chewing; but there is no bite in the cake.

Red Dwarf

The End
Rimmer and Lister walk back into the teaching room after seeing The Cat for the first time. Lister bumps into the table from which he was eating the piles of human ash – but all the ash has disappeared.

Royle Family, The

Christmas Special 1999
When Barbara gives Nana a snowball to drink, watch carefully as Nana talks about her late husband and you will see that the amount of liquid in her glass keeps changing between shots.

Seinfeld

The Dinner Party

Jerry takes one bite of the cookie but the bite size keeps changing between shots, without him ever taking another bite.

When Jerry is eating the black and white cookie in the bakery, sometimes the vanilla side is on the left and sometimes it is on the right. It keeps switching between shots.

The Opposite

Kramer is on the Regis and Kathie Lee show. After he puts up the coffee table, Kathie Lee has her coffee mug in her hand. In the next shot her hands are empty, and in the shot after that it's back in her hand again.

The Wife

When Meryl and Jerry are arguing over a can opener, a bottle of beer keeps changing positions whenever there's a cut back to Jerry.

Sex and the City

A Vogue Idea

When Carrie and the Vogue editor are drinking Martinis in his office, the level of liquor in their glasses changes from shot to shot.

Coulda, Woulda, Shoulda

Carrie is sitting at her laptop eating a blue ice pop. She takes a bite from the top then holds the stick with the rest of the ice pop between her teeth while she types on the laptop, and we see a shot of the screen. When we return to Carrie she is eating the rest of the ice pop off the stick, which is impossible because just two seconds before it was still attached to the stick. She didn't have time to bite it off the stick because she was using both her hands to type.

Catch-38

When Carrie and Charlotte are at the park, Carrie has a black and white cookie that keeps changing position in her hands with each shot of her. First the chocolate side is close to her, then it's away from her, then close again.

Simpsons, The

Homer vs. Lisa and the 8th Commandment

Marge gives Lisa a glass of 'lemonade'. It's orange. Weird lemons . . .

One Fish, Two Fish, Blowfish, Blue Fish

Homer eats and eats from his plate, but the same piece of food always reappears.

Principal Charming

While Skinner is admiring his tater tots, he is interrupted and lifts up his tray. As he inspects he tilts his tray to at least a 90-degree angle but everything, including the milk, stays exactly where it was.

Bart the Murderer

When Bart finds out that Homer took the police badge out of the cereal box, it changes from brown to pink. The food inside the box also changes to pink.

When we first see the papers on top of Skinner, the jar of preserves is not visible anywhere. It is beside him in the next shot.

Burns Verkaufen der Kraftwerk
When Homer hangs up on his stockbroker, the candy bar in Homer's right hand has disappeared.

When Lenny tells Homer he's the safety inspector, the doughnut and paper cup have disappeared from his hands.

Homer Defined
When all the salt spills out onto Milhouse's lunch, the salt that was on his food tray has disappeared.

There are many mistakes when Homer is checking for doughnut flavours, i.e. the positions of the doughnuts, the topping, etc.

Like Father, Like Klown
During the dinner scene, many things keep changing around, i.e. the glasses, the food, the silverware, etc.

Lisa's Pony
Lisa eats a spoonful of the ice cream and there is chocolate left over. The spoon suddenly changes to being clean.

Saturdays of Thunder
When Homer calls the Fatherhood Institute about his poor test results, the guy at the other end is holding a cup with 'Super Dad' on it. In the next three shots the cup has apparently jumped to a place on his desk.

In the scene where Homer laughs at Patty and Selma, for a few frames you can see that the beer can he was holding is gone. It stays beside the phone for the rest of the scene.

Separate Vocations

Near the beginning of the episode, when the family is eating dinner, the glasses on the table keep refilling and emptying themselves, even though nobody takes a drink.

After Bart gets promoted to hall monitor, when he tells the girl at the fountain to keep the line moving, the kid behind her drinks from the fountain but no water comes into his mouth.

In the scene at the beginning when the Simpsons are eating dinner, Marge and Homer's plates are empty, then they have food on them, then they are empty again

Tree House of Horror II: A Simpsons Halloween

Homer, Bart, Lisa and Maggie are eating sweets; they eat and eat and eat without taking the wrappers off.

When Flanders Failed

When the family is having dinner, the glasses on the table keep disappearing/reappearing between shots.

Rod and Todd Flanders are roasting marshmallows in the car. Todd's marshmallow was the only one above the lighter, even though both of them have turned black.

Deep Space Homer

Homer is in space and he is about to free the ants, but the crisps that he opened earlier have disappeared from the background.

Later, both the crisps and the ants disappear and reappear between shots.

Homer's Barbershop Quartet
Homer is talking to George Harrison and he sees that he has a brownie. He rushes over to a pile of brownies and starts scoffing them down. The pile of brownies doesn't get smaller.

The Boy Who Knew Too Much
Homer and Bart see each other skipping work/school. Homer, who is eating a doughnut, drops it on the pavement when he sees Bart. In the next shot of both of them the doughnut has disappeared.

A Star Is Burns
When the Simpson family and the TV Guy are having dinner, things like the food on their plates, their knives and forks, and even Homer's burping trophy disappear and then reappear for a couple of seconds before disappearing again.

Springfield Connection
When the Simpsons are eating and the family are praising Marge, Homer's plate is first seen to have a small amount of yellow food and a bit of pink food. In a later shot when Homer steals, and uses, Marge's pepper spray, he has a large pile of yellow food.

22 Short Films About Springfield
Skinner and the superintendent are having lunch; Skinner brings in four burgers. The superintendent takes one, and suddenly there is only one left.

Much Apu About Nothing

In the early scene where the Simpsons are gathered around the table to eat, you can see that they are eating slices of pie. However, in some of the long shots, the food on their plates changes and looks more like mashed potato and vegetables. Also, in the same scene, there's a shot of Lisa where you can see Bart's hand over her plate, but when the angle changes, it is behind her plate.

I, (Annoyed Grunt)-bot

When the family are eating dinner after the robot fight, their water glasses change position between shots.

Today, I Am a Klown

Homer writes an autograph for Ralph at the restaurant. Lisa is sitting opposite Marge and has yellow liquid in her glass and red and brown food on her plate. In the next shot, Lisa is opposite Homer and has a blue drink and white and green food.

Treehouse of Horror XIV

The piles of sweets and candy that Bart and Lisa have at the start vanish in the wide shots when Homer arrives.

South Park

Scott Tenorman Must Die

Cartman is eating his chilli; he almost empties the bowl before he stops to talk. The shot moves to Scott then back to Cartman and the bowl is seen to be almost full again with a little chilli sticking up above the brim.

Will & Grace

Last Ex to Brooklyn

As Leo speaks with Diane (he's on the sofa; she's in a chair) she refills her wine glass until it is nearly full. In the next shot Diane takes the last sip of wine from her glass, and the following shot shows her glass nearly full again.

RUN THAT PAST ME AGAIN

This last category is more of a general 'bizarre' group, with plot holes, odd character decisions, and stuff which plain makes no sense. Perhaps the programme makers hoped we wouldn't be thinking too much . . .

24

Day 2: 3:00 A.M.–4:00 A.M.

At about 3.10 a.m. the guys pick up Kate and head to her house. They arrive at 3.44 a.m., the same time that Jack leaves Yusaf. However, Jack arrives at Kate's house before the end of the episode, meaning he managed the drive in less than half the time of the other people. Sure, he was speeding, but the kidnappers were driving quickly too.

Alias

Endgame

Francie alters Will's cellphone so she can download items from the CIA's computers that are using it. In order to start the link, she calls him on the cellphone, asks him to look up a recipe on his computer, and then this cellphone is somehow able to download a three-gigabyte file. The phone Will uses has a maximum data transfer rate of 14.4 kbs; wouldn't Will get suspicious after he's forced to surf for this recipe for 57 hours while that gigantic file downloads?

Angel

Five By Five

In the scene where Angel tries to work out where Wesley is

being held hostage we learn that the man Faith beat up is still alive in the hospital and that it's his apartment she's staying in. A couple of scenes later Angel bursts into the apartment to save the day, but considering he's a vampire, and always needs to be invited into someone's home, how is this possible? As we've seen in other episodes, if the owner is alive, he should be barred from entering, even if the owner isn't actually in the apartment.

Angel finds Faith by tracking her to the apartment of the man whose wallet and keys she has stolen. The problem is that there's absolutely no way the police wouldn't have used this method to track down Faith themselves. There is no sign of the police until the disturbance of Angel and Faith fighting gets them interested.

There's No Place Like Plrtz Glrb

At the end of the episode, Angel Investigations come back from Pylea in the car and they end up in the club Caritas, but how did they manage to get the car out of the club in one piece? The only way out is through normal, narrow doors, and they're still using the car in Season Three.

Conviction (1)

Considering that Spike never visited Sunnydale or LA during Wesley's tenure in either place, how does Wesley recognise him straightaway? Giles' research in *Buffy* turned up no info, and he's more experienced than Wesley, so it makes no sense.

Boy Meets World

The Fugitive

When Amy and Morgan enter Cory's bathroom, Shawn somehow gets out (presumably through a window). But in 'Hair Today, Goon

Tomorrow', the bathroom is shown, and there is no window. So how did he escape from the bathroom in the earlier episode?

Buffy the Vampire Slayer

Becoming Part 1

According to Giles in 'Revelations' there are twelve cemeteries in Sunnydale, but in 'Becoming' Part 1, Buffy agrees to meet Angelus in 'the cemetery'. If there are twelve in the city, how would he ever know which one she means? (This is not the only time this error happens. In 'Smashed', for example, Spike does the same, asking Buffy to meet him at the cemetery.)

The Dark Age

Cordelia tells the Scoobies that Giles was talking to the police about a homicide, but this wasn't mentioned while she was in the room, so how does she know anything about it?

Anne

Ken tells Buffy that time in his hell dimension passes more quickly, that one day on Earth is the same as a hundred years in his dimension. This means time goes roughly 36,000 times quicker. When Lily falls into the portal, it's at least ten seconds until Buffy jumps in after her, but Lily is still just sitting there looking stunned. If time moves that much faster, ten seconds would become over four days. Would Lily still have been just sitting there?

Triangle

Anya says in this episode that she has never driven before, but in 'Graduation Day' Part 1 she tells Xander she has her car right outside. What did she do, push it there?

EastEnders

Across whole show

After Nana Moon has had brain surgery to help treat her memory loss, it's amazing she isn't missing a single hair from her head. If she had really had surgery she would have had the hair removed from at least part of her head.

Family Guy

Death Is a Bitch

As the plane is plummeting to the earth and Peter is talking to the Dawson kids and flight attendant Karen Black, from the way the plane is falling the people should either be on the floor or pressed up against the door to the cockpit. As it is, they are all just standing there as though the plane were flying on the level.

Friends

The One with the Dozen Lasagnes

Monica has to get rid of the lasagnes because they contain meat. However, when Rachel comes back into the apartment after dumping Paolo, Phoebe is eating a lasagne with Monica, even though she is a vegetarian.

The One with Two Parts: Part 2

When Monica is filling out Rachel's medical information, she has to change the name on the form so Rachel can use her insurance. You can see that she has a pencil in her hand. However, she goes up to the desk to get a new form. It makes no sense that she would arouse suspicion when all she has to do is erase Rachel's name and replace it with hers.

The One with Frank, Jr

Chandler tries to open the door that leads to his room, but Joey has sawed the door in half so only the upper half opens, and Chandler then falls over the bottom half. Why does the bottom half stick to the doorframe? He has to hit it with some force to fall over it, but it doesn't budge an inch.

The One with All the Thanksgivings

Monica is cheering up Chandler by putting a turkey on her head. Where did the whole uncooked turkey come from though, considering they had just had their meal? Did Monica just happen to have a large turkey in her freezer? To make matters worse, it is not possible for a human being to put a frozen turkey over their head for that long and not faint.

The One with Monica's Boots

Joey finds out that his younger sister Deena is pregnant. He then storms off and manages to find her boyfriend Bobby. How would he be able to, though? It is made clear that Joey has never met Bobby before, therefore he would not know what he looks like or where to find him. Even if he did somehow manage to find him, how did he manage to do it so quickly?

The One with the Red Sweater

On the night of the wedding, Joey kept ordering porn to everybody's hotel room and stealing nuts from their minibars. Where was everybody during the night (and especially the newlyweds)?

The One in Barbados, Part 1

Ross's computer is an Apple Powerbook G4. But Chandler opened up an infected email that contains the Anna Kournikova virus – it only affects Windows PCs.

M*A*S*H

Mad Dogs and Servicemen

Hawkeye, Henry and Trapper are playing Scrabble. The board is in an illegal state – in the lower right corner 'it', 'jot', 'joy', 'yearn' and 'in' are not connected to the rest of the words. Since the others call Hawkeye on his non-existent word, I'm assuming they're playing properly.

Movie Tonight

Radar impersonates John Wayne, playing a scene from *McClintock* – a film which was not released until 1963, which is ten years after the end of the Korean War.

Red Dwarf

Timeslides

We are told that it is impossible to move outside the frame of a slide, yet when we are shown the slide of young Lister and his band, all we see is the band on stage, but the crew move freely about the pub.

After Lister manages to make himself the inventor of the tension sheet, Rimmer is in the sleeping quarters and Lister's bunk can be seen behind him, still like it was. If Lister was never on Red Dwarf then why is all his stuff still in his bunk and on the walls?

After the crew return from giving young Lister the tension sheet, Lister, The Cat and Kryten disappear because Lister had now never joined the crew. Rimmer should also disappear or be replaced by McIntyre, because his hologram was created for the sole purpose of keeping Lister sane.

Justice

The justice computer states that Rimmer is guilty of 1167 counts of second-degree murder, each carrying a sentence of 8 years giving a total of 9328 years. But this is equivalent to 1166 counts.

Back to Reality

When the crew are in the recuperation lounge, a woman comes in and asks if anyone in the room is called Dwayne Dibley. After everyone denies that it could be them, the woman leaves the case for someone to look at. After she leaves, Lister looks at the case and says it has to be The Cat because his photograph is on the case. If this is so, then why did the woman not just look at the picture and tell for herself who Dwayne was instead of repeatedly asking?

Demons & Angels

In 'White Hole', everything that happened, including the pool game, was erased from the crew's memories. So how does Lister remember 'playing pool with planets' in this episode?

Seinfeld

The Airport

Jerry is upgraded to first class while Elaine struggles in coach. The scene changes to show a plane flying with the colours of Southwest Airlines, but that airline doesn't have a first class.

Simpsons, The

The Telltale Head

After leaving the Kwik-e-Mart, Bart asks the bad kids where they got all their great stuff. Jimbo says, 'Five finger discount.' But they only have four fingers.

Flaming Moe's

As Homer watches TV at the beginning of this episode, look really closely and you will see that the remote on the couch is exactly the same colour (brown) as the sofa. It disappears after a while, and then reappears later.

Lisa's Pony

At the beginning of the talent show, Skinner tells the audience that all the doors are locked. Homer enters the auditorium during Lisa's performance.

Guess Who's Coming to Criticise Dinner

The keyboard that Homer uses to write his report doesn't have a working E key. When his boss looks at it he says that he repeats 'screw Flanders' at the end. Screw Flanders has two E's.

Star Trek

The Naked Time

Spock starts to lose control of his emotions and is desperately struggling with himself. He goes towards a room and the automatic doors open for him. As they close behind him, Spock leans back against the doors. The doors should sense something approaching and open again, depositing our heroic Vulcan on his back in the corridor.

Star Trek: The Next Generation

The Next Phase

Geordi and Ro are made intangible through contact with an experimental shield generator. They pass through all solid objects but for some reason are still able to stand on the decks of the ship. On several occasions they and the Romulan in the same situation pass through the walls but not the floors of the *Enterprise*. Can't be the gravity generators or they'd be pulled through the floor of the upper decks.

Star Trek: Voyager

Elogium

In this episode Kes states that she has to decide now whether to have a child or not because Ocampa women can only get pregnant once and deliver one child. If that was the case they would have died out a long time ago, or never even evolved as two people only getting one offspring would reduce the population to fifty per cent of the original figure each generation.

Will & Grace

Sex, Losers and Videotape

Grace is trying her damnedest to make a sexy video to send to Leo – why? He's working on a viral outbreak in sub-Saharan Africa, and he told Grace in an earlier episode, 'these people don't have running water.' Doesn't make sense that his precious cargo of food and medicine would include a VCR, even if electricity is on hand.

INDEX